metal clay
& color

INVENTIVE
TECHNIQUES
FROM **20**
JEWELRY
DESIGNERS

compiled by
Mary Wohlgemuth

D1319422

KB
KALMBACH BOOKS

Kalmbach Books
21027 Crossroads Circle
Waukesha, Wisconsin 53186
www.Kalmbach.com/Books

© 2012 Kalmbach Books

All rights reserved. Except for brief excerpts for review, this book may not be reproduced in part or in whole by electronic means or otherwise without written permission of the publisher.

The jewelry designs in *Metal Clay & Color* are the copyrighted property of the designers, and they may not be taught or sold without permission. Please use them for your education and personal enjoyment only.

Published in 2012
16 15 14 13 12   1 2 3 4 5

Manufactured in the United States of America

ISBN: 978-0-87116-441-4

Editor: Mary Wohlgemuth
Art Director: Lisa Bergman
Technical Editor: Jill L. Erickson
Illustrator: Kellie Jaeger
Photographers: James Forbes, William Zuback

Library of Congress Cataloging-in-Publication Data
Metal clay & color : inventive techniques from 20 jewelry designers / compiled by Mary Wohlgemuth ; [foreword by Celie Fago].

 p. : ill. (chiefly col.) ; cm.

ISBN: 978-0-87116-441-4

1. Jewelry making–Handbooks, manuals, etc. 2. Precious metal clay–Coloring–Handbooks, manuals, etc. I. Wohlgemuth, Mary. II. Fago, Celie. III. Title: Metal clay and color

TT212 .M48 2012
739.275

Contents

Considering color

MY EARLIEST MEMORIES about color are of my father at his drafting desk, working into the wee hours of the night with the stains of Dr. Martin's colored inks on his hands, and of my mother, a "modern artist," furiously painting whenever she managed to slip our familial grasp. My father used color to illustrate graphics; my mother used color to describe form. Shifting between their very different approaches helped me develop a unique perspective.

Whether it was sitting on the kitchen floor drawing with a fat crayon or sewing leaf tapestries with a threaded thorn apple spine in the woods, I was learning the ropes of this family business of art and laying the foundation for my life's work.

In art school, I studied printmaking, sculpture, and painting. My greatest lesson came in an exercise from my painting instructor: For six months, I could use only my two least-favorite colors, orange and turquoise, in my work. It was torture for the first few months. But I was forced to think differently about those two colors, and eventually all colors, and to become more circumspect about my choices.

The lesson led to a greater self-awareness about the process I used for translating my ideas into art. It also helped me understand color in a broader sense: how to look at color and how to look at paintings.

In 1990, a friend sent me a handful of brightly colored buttons. They were made of polymer clay and I was transfixed. The three-dimensionality and small scale suited me far better than painting, and the fact that the form and color were in the same material fascinated me. I began making jewelry in polymer clay and mixing metal with it soon after. Polymer seemed too light by itself; I felt it needed metal to add both aesthetic and actual weight to the polymer. I spent the next several years zealously learning metalworking and finding ways to combine the two materials.

Later that decade, a truly revolutionary material changed everything—for me and for many others. It was metal; it was clay; it was amazing! For a long, intense period following that discovery, the only color in my work came from the subtle hues of patina on fine silver created with a tiny bit of a liver of sulfur gravel in lukewarm water.

As I gained fluency with metal clay, I began adding other materials and using traditional metalwork to combine them: polymer, colored pencils, 24k gold keum-boo, found objects, brass, bronze, copper, and old tin. The point is perspective:

Carved bracelets, 2010. *A little bit of everything is used—polymer, seed beads, and various colors of metal clay. Photo by Robert Diamante.*

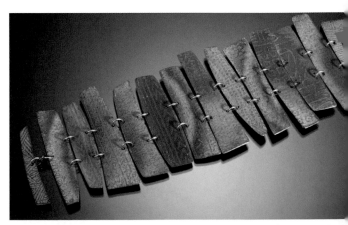

Fencepost bracelet, 2009. *Bronze clay brought a new wave of unexpected color: a serendipitous patina produced by the coal carbon firing. Photo by Robert Diamante.*

Open locket, 2007. *Paper made with my tearaway technique became the framed images and was used as the texturing tool for the silver clay as well. Photo by Robert Diamante.*

Working back and forth between polymer clay and metal… or paint and PMC … silver wire and colored thread … oil crayons and pure gold … or bronze, copper, and cut tin … all this interplay gives me ever-changing, invaluable reference points.

It's a special challenge to use color—or, perhaps, to use color well—in the confines of the usually tiny format of jewelry, as presented in the projects that follow. A little goes a long way.

Today I am aware of a sort of restlessness with regard to color that keeps pushing me forward, for better or worse, toward different means and ways of adding color to my work. Each new material or process influences the way I see the work, and thus the direction I take. It's inevitable that using metal in clay form would change the way I view my choices in making art.

But color is the constant, and learning to approach color with equal parts of caution and wild abandon is always time well spent.

With that in mind, I hope color tempts you into new directions for your metal clay work. Take advantage of the lovely compendium of ideas in this book. Use the techniques, combine them, or let them kindle a new idea of your own. Enjoy!

Cameo pendant, 2008. *One of my favorite ways of working with color is to make a cameo of color and design to set in a format such as a ring or a pendant. As I make these tiny paintings, I apply the same principles I use in painting in large scale.*

After texturing polymer clay with an etched polymer-and-paper plate made with the tearaway technique, I rub acrylic, oil paint, or oil crayons into its surface. After baking and then fixing the color with liquid polymer, I cut out the cameo and set it into a metal clay piece. Making this work in an inch of space without making mud is challenging. Imagine how a pendant is seen—both at a hand's breadth and from a conversational distance of 3–6 feet. Photo by Douglas Foulke.

Patinas are notoriously unpredictable and should be explored in that spirit. I get a deep mottled red on copper by fluxing it, heating it with a torch until it glows, and then plunging it into boiling water. Different fluxes change the outcome, as does using ice-cold instead of boiling water. This piece shows fine silver riveted onto copper sheet.

I use the same technique—heating with a torch and plunging into boiling water—to intensify the color of pieces made from copper clay.

Bronze goes bright blue when suspended over household ammonia in a tight glass jar for hours or days.

All photos above by Jennifer Kahn.

Introduction

WHEN ITS JAPANESE INVENTORS unveiled metal clay in the mid-1990s, there was much to be learned about the medium. Metal clay fascinated artists everywhere. Today the same explorers and innovators, joined by many others, are pushing the boundaries of combining other materials with their metal clay as part of the natural evolution of a young artistic medium. It's no surprise that many of the elements being added today involve color—whether brilliant or subtle, stunning or simple.

Color in its many forms complements and enlivens the beauty of metal tones. And today, with the development of many new varieties of metal clay, the color of the metal itself takes many forms—bright fine silver, mellow sterling silver, warm bronze and copper, and even cool steel.

This book celebrates and shares the work of 20 prominent artists working in the medium who are known for their explorations of color with metal clay. The secondary media that provide the exciting color element of each piece include alcohol inks, cement, ceramic clay, colored pencil, dye oxides, enamel, fireable gemstones, Gilders paste, glass, metal clay in various forms (gold, copper, silver, steel), metal leaf, polymer, resin, sand, and seed beads.

The Artists Gallery images throughout the book suggest even more applications to stir your imagination: Scraps of tin, felted wool, and even discarded CDs can provide a shot of color alongside metal. These images showcase the work of the book's contributing designers as well as 14 other talented artists.

How to use this book

The projects in this book span a wide range of skill levels, from beginner to advanced, and they are presented in that order. Because the focus is on the application of color into metal clay, designers were asked to emphasize that aspect of the project, and thus some fundamental metal clay construction instructions may be condensed. If you are new to metal clay, learning some metal clay basics including construction techniques from a class or a book may be helpful (see p. 111 for a suggestion).

To create the projects, you'll need a basic setup for working with metal clay, which is detailed on the facing page. Each project lists additional supplies needed. Tinted boxes labeled "Color" give a list of the special materials, supplies, and tools that will be needed to work with the color medium that's explored in each project.

New metal clay formulas and products are introduced regularly. Although we have tried to be as complete and up-to-date as possible in the instructions, please refer to the manufacturer's instructions for working with and firing the specific type of metal clay you use.

You'll find background information on all of the contributing designers starting on p. 109 and tips for sourcing unusual project supplies on p. 111.

METAL CLAY THICKNESS GUIDE

Measurement	Slat color	Playing card(s)
.25mm		1
.5mm		2
.75mm		3
1mm		4
1.5mm		6
2mm		8

Metal clay toolkit

Wet clay tools and supplies
- Nonstick work surface (flexible Teflon sheet)
- Olive oil or natural hand balm
- Distilled water and plastic spray bottle
- PVC tube or acrylic roller
- Thickness gauge slats or playing cards
- Cutting tools: craft knife or scalpel, tissue blade, shaped cutters
- Rubber-tipped shaping and smoothing tools (clay shapers)
- Clear, acrylic rolling rectangle
- Drinking straws
- Needle tool
- Fine-tip paintbrush
- Texture sheets, stamps, and molds
- Tweezers
- Spatula or palette knife
- Airtight storage containers
- Plastic wrap
- Sponges
- Mug warmer

Dry clay tools and supplies
- Rubber block
- Needle files*
- Pin vise, drill bits
- Emery boards in various grits*
- Sandpaper or flexible sanding pads in various grits*
- Polishing papers*
- Mini/micro carving tools
- Containers to store dry and reconstituted clay*

Keep separate sets of these items for each type of clay (fine silver, sterling silver, copper, bronze, steel, etc.)

Firing and finishing tools
- Kiln and kiln shelf
- Kiln-safe gloves
- Eye protection
- Dust mask (when using vermiculite and fiber blanket)
- Vermiculite
- Fiber blanket
- Stainless steel lidded container and activated carbon or coconut shell carbon*
- Kiln stilts*
- Brass- or steel-bristle brush
- Steel or agate burnisher
- Tumbler, stainless steel shot, burnishing compound
- Liver of sulfur or other patina solutions, glass containers
- Baking soda
- Polishing cloth

Required for firing the following clays: sterling silver, copper, bronze, and steel

General safety guidelines

- Wear a dust mask while working with materials and tools that generate particulates.
- Read all Material Safety Data Sheets (MSDSs) before using a new material, and keep a copy of the MSDS for any material you use.
- Do not use tools or chemicals in ways that are contrary to the manufacturer's intended purpose.
- Wear protective gloves while handling caustic materials or chemicals.
- Keep a properly rated fire extinguisher and a source of clean water near your workstation.
- Keep cutting tools sharp and all tools and equipment properly maintained.
- Dedicate all tools to nonfood use.

Kiln and firing safety guidelines

- Use your kiln in a well-ventilated area.
- Follow manufacturers' instructions for programming your kiln and sintering times and temperatures.
- Do not torch-fire metal clay pieces that have a core inclusion, such as cork or wood clay.
- Do not sinter or torch-fire metal clay pieces that are not completely dry, as they may explode.

Projects

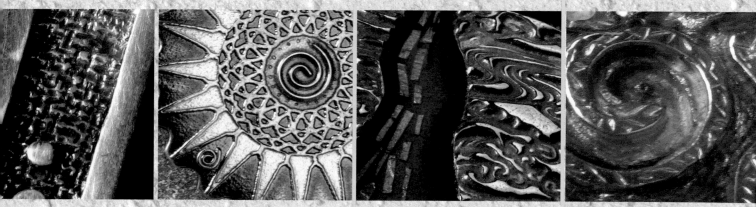

DESIGNER **Lorrene Baum-Davis**

Easy keum-boo

The keum-boo technique is an inexpensive way to add the luster of high-karat gold to fine-silver clay. This technique was used primarily by Asian artisans for adhering gold to steel, copper, and iron. Its re-emergence in Western art has brought forth amazing applications of this precious metal to our art forms. In this project, as an alternative to using a hot plate, I use a handheld butane torch to apply gold foil to the metal.

color

Medium/technique
Torch-fired keum-boo

Tools & supplies
• Sheet of gold foil or gold leaf
• Scissors
• Handheld butane torch
• Charcoal block
• Thick fiber blanket or
  soldering pad
• Sharp-point tweezers
• Burnishers: agate, steel

Metal clay
• Fired fine-silver jewelry piece

Metal clay toolkit (p. 7)

Prepare the metal clay component

The surface of your fired fine-silver component must be free of all oils, chemicals, and burnishing compound prior to applying the gold leaf. If you are making a new metal clay piece for this project, allow it to air cool after it is fired and don't touch it with your fingers. Leave the piece unburnished; this will help the gold foil adhere better.

If your fine-silver piece has been handled, burnished, or tumble-polished, use a handheld butane torch to heat the metal until the surface has the white look of a freshly kiln-fired piece.

Prepare the gold foil

Genuine gold leaf is metal that has been hammered or milled to a very thin sheet. Gold foil is a thicker version, which I prefer for keum-boo. A sheet of gold leaf can be folded a few times to create a thicker layer.

Gold leaf and gold foil sheets are typically packaged between sheets of tissue paper. Use a paper clip to hold the gold foil sheet in the tissue paper, draw your chosen design on the paper, and use scissors to cut out the pattern [A]. You can also use paper punches to cut out precise shapes. Place the cut pieces on a stone slab or dish.

Keum-boo station

Place a charcoal block on a thick fiber blanket or soldering pad on your work surface. Place the fired and cooled fine-silver component on the block. Use sharp tweezers to transfer a cut piece of foil to the silver piece. Make sure your handheld butane torch and steel and agate burnishers are within reach.

Light the butane torch to a low bushy flame and aim it at the top of the charcoal block, taking care not to allow the force of the flame to displace the gold foil. Hold the foil in place with the steel burnisher in your dominant hand as you slowly heat the metal, moving the torch flame in a circular motion [B]. Turn off the torch and set it aside.

While the metal is hot, use the agate burnisher to press the gold onto the silver, working from the center outward. I like to use the steel burnisher to hold the metal in place as I burnish with the agate burnisher [C]. If the agate burnisher begins to pull or stick to the foil, switch to the steel burnisher. You can quench a steel burnisher in water to cool it.

Do not quench agate burnishers in water—the thermal shock can cause the stone to crack.

If the foil is not fully adhered to the metal, reheat the metal while simultaneously holding the gold foil in place with the steel burnisher. Then repeat the burnishing process until the foil is bonded to the metal.

Repeat these steps to apply any remaining gold foil to the metal.

Finishing options

You can burnish the metal to a high shine with a brass-bristle brush [D]. Or use the steel burnisher to polish only the high points of the metal, leaving the recessed areas with a matte finish.

If desired, apply a liver of sulfur patina to the metal. Remove excess patina with a brass brush or polishing cloth.

Depletion gilding sterling silver

If you'd like to try the keum-boo technique on a sterling silver piece rather than fine silver, you'll have to raise a layer of fine silver on its surface due to its copper content. This is called depletion gilding. Use a torch to heat the metal until black oxides form on its surface. Quench and pickle the metal to remove the oxides. Repeat the process of heating, quenching, and pickling until the surface no longer turns black when heated with the torch.

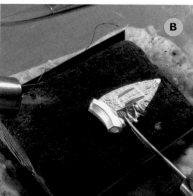

DESIGNER **Susan Breen Silvy**

Full-spectrum impact

If you are looking for controllable, high-impact hues, adding dye oxides to your toolkit may be the answer. Dye oxides create patinas that are interesting, fairly inexpensive, and require minimal investment in tools. You can achieve a full spectrum of colors with these colorants, from pastels to deep jewel tones that range from transparent to opaque.

color

Medium/technique
Dye oxides

Tools & supplies
- Water
- Isopropyl alcohol
- Dye oxide patinas: blue-green, green, and pea green
- Paintbrush
- Cosmetic swabs*
- Distilled water
- Non-contact infrared thermometer
- 2 dishes or jars of water
- Paper towels
- Several eyedroppers
- Painters palette or plastic medicine cups
- Natural-bristle paintbrushes in small and medium sizes
- Permalac spray lacquer

These are like firm cotton swabs; find them in the makeup section of a drugstore. One end is pointed and the other has a flattened, round end.

Metal clay
- 16 grams fine-silver clay OR
- Fired, tumbled, and polished metal clay jewelry piece

Metal clay toolkit (p. 7)

Additional tools & supplies
- Card stock or index cards

About dye oxides

My research into colorants for metal clay started with solvent dyes, which gave me the desired effect but were temperamental to work with and required solvent thinner—definitely messy and sometimes dangerous. My experiments eventually led me to water-based dye oxide patinas, which give me the same, if not better, results. The colors are transparent and can be blended or layered to achieve the effect you're after. They do not contain acids and can be thinned with distilled water. Although still a bit messy, accidents can be cleaned up with a damp rag—a huge benefit.

These directions are for making a simple pendant, which has ample surface for experimenting with blending colors as well as raised areas that you will want to leave free of color. You can also use any fired, tumbled, and polished piece you like. If you are careful and touch only the outside framework, you will not have to worry about cleaning the surface that will be accepting the dye oxides. For your first piece, it is best to use fine-silver clay, since it is easier to see the color change with silver as the background.

Dye oxides are best applied to metal that is 180–200°F (82–92°C). A mug warmer works beautifully. Different areas of the heated plate can reflect different temperatures, so a noncontact infrared thermometer is an important tool to have on hand.

It is easiest to begin with a piece that lies flat on the mug warmer. If you apply a bail on the back, you will have to hold the piece steady with tweezers while applying the color, which can be distracting when you are learning how to use the dyes.

If your finished piece has a deep recess where you will apply the dyes, you will be able to concentrate on what the dyes are doing, not where they are going. As you become more proficient in working with the materials, you'll be able to comfortably apply them to areas with less relief.

Make the metal clay pendant
To make the templates, cut two 1½ x ½" (38 x 13mm) rectangles from card stock or index cards. Cut a frame from one of the rectangles by marking and cutting ⅛" (3mm) inside the perimeter of the rectangle. Roll the clay to 3 cards/.75mm thick. Cut around the frame template and cut three small circles (or dots) of various sizes for the center embellishment. Cut the back plate from a lightly textured slab of clay 3 cards thick. Set all pieces aside to dry **[A]**. You can set a small, fireable stone in the middle of one of the dots if desired.

Assemble the dry pieces by priming the area with water, adding slip to the back of the frame, and affixing it to the textured side of the back plate. Decide where you want the circles, allowing room between elements so you can get a small brush between them to add the dye oxides. Set aside to dry.

Seal the outside edges of the pendant by priming with water and "caulking"

generously with fresh clay between the layers. Set aside to dry.

Sand the sides, making sure the corners form crisp 90-degree angles. Fill any cracks and prefinish your piece using whatever method you prefer for creating a shiny finish. Decide where you will make a chain connection and drill holes for jump rings **[B]**.

Don't leave any sanding marks or scratches on the area that you plan to leave shiny. The dye loves to seep into small scratches, where it concentrates while the water in the solution evaporates. Removing dye from small scratches is almost impossible, requiring it to suddenly become a "design element."

Fire, brass-brush, and tumble the metal clay piece until it is shiny. Work on the edges around the interior of the frame to make sure everything has a nice finish. The shiny surface will reflect through the transparent dye oxides, which is one of the best aspects of using this process. If the silver remains matte, the color will have a dull, matte look.

Don't touch the textured part of the pendant where the dye oxides will go, because skin oils can repel the solution. If you do accidentally touch it, clean the area with isopropyl alcohol and a swab. Put the tumbled piece on a mug warmer or in a dehydrator. I use a dehydrator set at 155°F (68°C) for a couple of hours to dry the clay. Metal clay is porous; make sure that all water within it has evaporated and won't interfere with the patina.

Apply the dye oxides
Preheat the mug warmer for 15–20 minutes. Prepare the dye oxides. Shake the bottles well, making sure all the oxides are

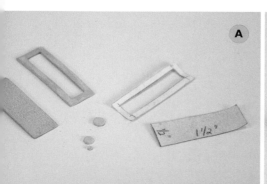
A

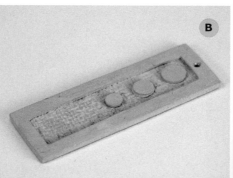
B

C

suspended. I shake all the colors that I know I am going to use and then shake them again just before I measure them out.

Prepare your work area. Set out the small plastic cups or artist palette, tweezers, paintbrushes, eyedropper, infrared thermometer, and two cups of water. One cup is for washing off the brush between colors, and the second cup is a final rinse for the brush to make sure none of the previous patina remains in the bristles [C].

Place the pendant on the mug warmer. Shake the dye oxides and use an eyedropper to place a small amount of each color into the wells of the palette [D]. Check the temperature of the pendant to make sure it's around 200°F (93°C) [E]. My pendant was too hot, so I moved it to the edge of the mug warmer, where it was cooler. When the pendant reaches temperature, load a paintbrush with blue-green and start applying it to the bottom third of the textured area [F].

Your goal is a blended color from blue through green to yellow. Subtly feather the color into the middle third of the textured area where the green will be placed. Dip the brush into water and apply the diluted oxide to the area, feathering it toward the middle third of the texture. After the solution

dries, if you want a deeper color, load the brush again, brush the same area with another coat of dye, and follow with a brush of water. Don't worry if you slop onto the side frame area or the dots; you can clean it up later.

With a clean brush, repeat the color application and feathering using green in the middle third of the textured area. Feather the green down into the blue-green and into the top third [G]. Remember to dip your brush in water so you have a diluted solution to subtly feather the color. Occasionally check on the temperature of your pendant and make any adjustments necessary to keep it in the suggested range.

With a clean brush, repeat the feathering technique in the top third of the textured area [H]. When the pea green is a depth of color you like, give the entire textured piece a thin coating of pea green to help pull all the colors together. Place the pendant on the mug warmer for a few minutes and then move it to the dehydrator set to 155°F (68°C) for about 5 minutes. The patina will continue to develop in the warmth. If you don't have a dehydrator, just keep the piece on the mug warmer for 15 minutes or so. This is the easiest step of all: Ignore your pendant until the next day.

Don't leave the mug warmer unattended. And don't forget to shut it off between work sessions!

Clean the work
Using a slightly dampened makeup swab, gently clean any mishaps that may have happened when applying the dye oxides. Gently swab the entire perimeter of the piece, checking the swab occasionally [I]. You'll be able to see the patina on the swab more easily than on the silver piece. So if you notice color on the swab, using a clean area of the swab, go over that area again until the swab comes away clean. Keep in mind that any patina that is left in a place you didn't intend will be permanently sealed in a later step.

Avoid touching the textured patina area. It is very easy to accidentally swipe an area with the wet swab or smear it with your fingers; the patina is still very delicate. When you are finished removing the unwanted splatter, pop the piece back into the dehydrator for a few minutes to make sure it is completely dry.

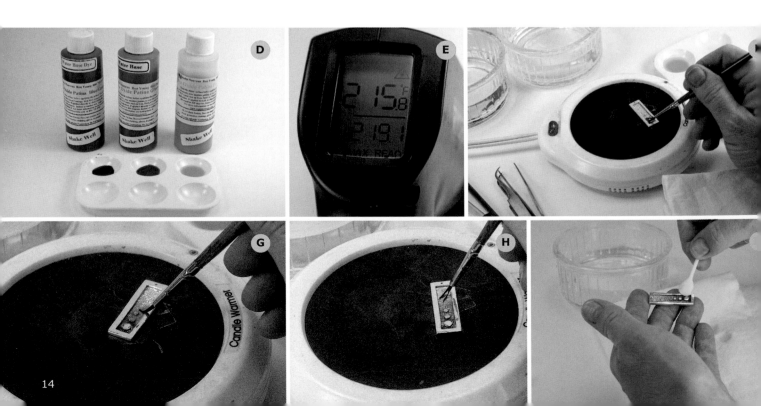

Joy Funnell, Having a Hoot, 2011. Fine silver, enamel. Photo by the artist.

Michela Verani, Dr. Seuss Ring, 2011. Fine silver, felt, seed beads. Photo by Jessica Healy.

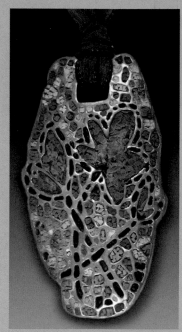

Cindy Silas, Mountain Meadow, 2011. Bronze, polymer. Photo by the artist.

Seal the patina

Set up an area (perhaps outside) where you can spray your piece with spray lacquer.

I have tried other spray lacquers from jewelry suppliers, but I recommend only Permalac. It is an amazingly hard lacquer and is recommended by the manufacturers of the dye oxide patinas.

If you have added a gemstone to your pendant, cover the stone with a small piece of tape to protect it from the spray. Wipe your piece with a soft cloth to remove any fingerprints or dust.

You will spray your pendant with two or three light coats of lacquer. Place your work on something that will absorb the overspray. I spray on old cardboard or scraps of art board. You do not want the spray to accumulate around the edge of the piece or you will have an ugly, lumpy mess at the edges. Don't use something like wax paper or plastic that will bead up the overspray and then dry on your piece.

Let the lacquer dry for 20–30 minutes between coats. Run your finger gently over the area with color. If any color is evident on your fingertip, you have missed a spot and need to apply another coat or two of sealer.

Move the pendant to a dust-free spot so the sealer can cure for a couple of days. Give the sealer ample time to bond with the patina and metal.

Care instructions

Jewelry with a dye oxide patina should be cleaned with a soft, dry cloth; never use a sonic cleaner or submerge it in water. If it's unusually dirty, use a slightly damp cloth.

Consider setting a small, fireable gemstone in the center of one of the dots for an extra kick of color.

Filled frame beads

These beads have a lot of flair, but they don't use a lot of silver clay. The basic structure uses a sterling silver frame or shape that is pierced for threading. Prefabricated bead frames provide an easy starting point, although any shape can be constructed from strip. Polymer clay that is layered mokume-gane style provides the color and fills the structure. I've used various other polymer techniques with this style of bead, including faux stones, faux ivory, and canework.

color

Medium/technique
Polymer clay

Tools & supplies
• 3 colors of polymer clay (I used Premo! Sculpey Black, Wasabi, and a mix of 1 part white and 2 parts Pearl)
• Tissue blade
• Spray bottle
• Fine needle or quilting pen

Metal clay
• 12–15 grams fine-silver clay

Metal clay toolkit (p. 7)

Additional tools & supplies
• Sculpey SuperFlex Bake & Bend clay (to make texture sheets)
• Ball stylus tool
• Craft oven
• 5 prefabricated circular sterling silver bead frames, 4 x 22mm
• Circle cutters, 20mm and 27mm*
• Sanding pad for use with dry metal clay
• Fine, flat metal file
• Easy paste solder
• Butane torch
• Soldering pad
• Pickle solution (I use a citric acid pickle in a warming pot)
• Chain, wire, and clasp for finishing as desired

I use PMC3, and these sizes work exactly with the bead frames. If using a different brand or formula of metal clay, adjust for a different shrinkage factor.

Use the technique and the concept in other styles and shapes of jewelry.

I create my original texture sheets using Sculpey SuperFlex Bake & Bend clay—the most rubbery and flexible of all clay formulas. Using the same texture for the metal and the polymer elements provides a lovely visual echo.

Make the texture sheet

Roll about a quarter package of Bake & Bend clay into a sheet about 2mm thick. Using the ball stylus, draw a pattern in the clay **[A]**. (If you create any burs, wait until the piece is baked and shave them off with a clay blade.) Bake according to the manufacturer's instructions on the polymer clay package. Cool.

Texture and finish the metal clay

Roll the metal clay to a thickness of 3 cards/ .75mm. Oil the polymer texture sheet lightly and place it face down on the metal clay.

Roll firmly across the sheet in one direction. Peel away the texture sheet **[B]**. Using the 27mm cutter, cut five circles from the clay **[C]**.

Using the 20mm cutter, cut out a section of each circle to create crescent shapes **[D]**. Reroll the scrap clay and repeat if necessary to create five shapes. Vary the depth of the interior curves if desired. Dry the crescent shapes completely. Sand the surface and edges lightly to remove any burs and to smooth the pattern surface. Fire the metal clay with either a torch or kiln according to the manufacturer's recommendations. Burnish the surfaces with a brass-bristle brush.

Solder the bead frames

Apply a bead of paste solder around the lower edge of the bead frame where it will

contact the crescent shape. (Easy paste solder contains flux. If you use wire or sheet solder, dip the pieces in flux before heating.) The bead frame should sit just inside the outer edge of the crescent, but as close as possible to the edge without leaving gaps **[E]**. Heat with the torch until the solder flows throughout the join **[F]**. Cool. Clean the bead frames in pickle solution.

File the outer edge of the piece until the sterling strip and the fine-silver texture pattern appear to be a single smooth surface **[G]**. Add patina to the bead frames with liver of sulfur solution if desired. Polish the surface with a polishing pad to bring back the bright surface and highlight the texture **[H]**.

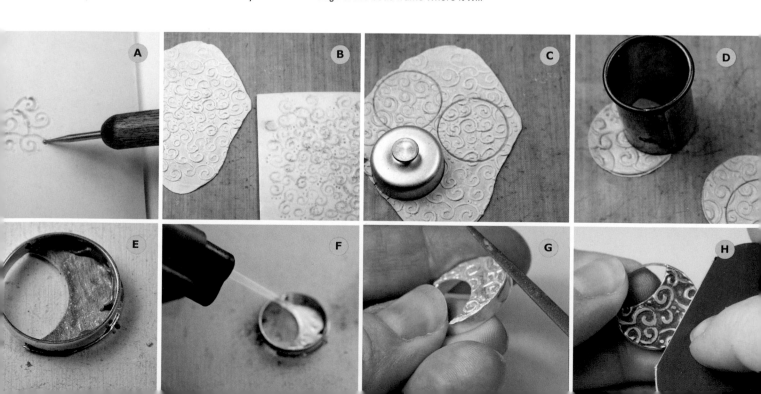

Create textured polymer and fill the frames

Roll about a sixth of each 2-oz. package of the three polymer clay colors into sheets of equal size. Use the thickest setting on a pasta machine or roll by hand to about ⅛" **[I]**. Stack the sheets **[J]**.

Roll the stack through the thickest setting on the pasta machine or roll by hand until the thickness of the three sheets is reduced to the original thickness. Cut the sheet in half and stack the two pieces **[K]**. Repeat the rolling and cutting process twice **[L]**.

Mist the surface of the texture sheet with water and roll it firmly against the layered polymer sheet. Repeat if the texture sheet is smaller than the overall surface. With the clay blade nearly parallel to the surface of the sheet, carefully shave the raised texture off the sheet **[M]**. When the sheet is completely shaved, roll to smooth the surface **[N]**. Fold the sheet in half with the pattern side out **[O]**.

Roll with the rod if necessary to thin the sheet. The sheet should be only slightly thicker than the depth of the bead frames. Place the bead frames on the surface, choosing the areas of pattern to show through the open spaces. Press them firmly to fill the space and cut the beads from the sheet **[P]**. Pierce the beads through the existing holes in the sterling frames using a fine needle or quilting pin **[Q]**. Bake the beads according to the manufacturer's instructions on the polymer clay package. Cool.

String the necklace

The example shown in the photo on p. 16 combines beads made of onyx, rhyolite, hematite, and sterling silver. It is strung on beading wire, finished with crimp beads, and it joins a length of chain at the back.

Metal leaf magic

The dry construction of this project enables you to make a beautiful double-sided pendant. The wells on the shell of this sweet sea turtle are the perfect place to add color using variegated metal leaf embedded in UV-cured resin.

color

Medium/technique
Metal leaf in resin

Tools & supplies
• UV-cure resin
• Variegated metal leaf
• Toothpicks
• UV lamp

Metal clay
• 40 grams fine-silver clay
• Paste clay
• Syringe clay

Metal clay toolkit (p. 7)

Additional tools & supplies
• Polymer clay for mold-making
• Card stock
• Turtle mold
• Fine-silver embeddable jump ring
• Fiber blanket
• Chain or cord for finishing as desired

I used a six-part mold for my turtle, but the technique is adaptable to any design with shallow wells to hold the metal leaf suspended in resin.

Make the drying forms

Press polymer clay into the top shell of the mold, trim around the edge, and bake according to the manufacturer's instructions on the polymer clay package. Cut card stock into 42 squares, each approximately ½" (13mm). Stack and tape together two stacks of 12 cards each and three stacks of 6 cards each [A].

Make the turtle parts

Roll 20 grams of metal clay to 8 cards/2mm thick. Press into the top shell section of the mold. The clay will thin out a bit during this step. Remove the clay from the mold, trim any excess clay, and smooth the edges with a moist paintbrush. Drape the shape over the polymer clay form to dry [B].

Roll the remaining metal clay to 8 cards thick and press it into the bottom shell mold. Dry flat. Press a 2-gram ball of metal clay into the head mold. Remove from the mold, trim the excess clay, and smooth with a moist paintbrush. Dry. File and sand smooth the top and bottom shell and the head with 600-grit sandpaper.

Roll 10 grams of metal clay to 8 cards thick. Press into front legs mold. Remove from the mold, trim the excess clay, and smooth the edges with a moist brush. Lightly drape the legs upside down over the underside of the dried top shell. Repeat for the back legs.

Center the dried head piece on the wet front legs and press to create a dent; leave in place. Dry using card stock drying forms:

Place the 12-layer card stacks under the front legs and the 6-layer card stacks under the back legs and the head [C]. Dry. Remove the legs from the shell, file, and sand.

Assemble the turtle

Using a generous amount of paste, attach the front and back legs and the head to the wrong side of the shell [D]. Let dry. Paste the bottom shell to the top shell. Embed a 4mm fine-silver jump ring between the head and the leg as shown [E]. Let dry.

Fill the gaps

Using a clay syringe with no tip attached, fill the gaps between the top and bottom shells [F]. Smooth with a paintbrush. Dry. Repeat and dry again until gaps are completely filled. File and sand. Using a file, carve lines

in the smooth gaps to extend the segments of the bottom shell [G].

Fire and add patina

Support the entire piece in fiber blanket. Fire according to the metal clay manufacturer's suggested firing time and temperature. Let cool. Burnish with a wire-bristle brush and tumble if desired. Use liver of sulfur solution to add patina. Polish as desired.

Adding the variegated metal leaf

Using tweezers, tear tiny pieces of the metal leaf and set aside [H]. Squeeze a ¾" (19mm) diameter puddle of resin onto a piece of paper. With a toothpick, place a very thin layer of resin in one of the shell segments [I]. Pick up a tiny piece of leaf and place it into the segment on the resin [J]. Repeat, adding resin and one piece of metal leaf to each shell segment. Place under a UV lamp for 5 minutes. Use the toothpick to add a drop of resin into each segment [K] until the whole shell is covered. Place the piece under the lamp until the resin is no longer tacky. Attach a jump ring to the bail and hang on a chain or cord.

I used the same color technique with one-part molds to make a simpler pendant and earrings.

J

K

Janet Alexander, Atlantis, 2011. Fine silver, alcohol ink. Photo by Marsha Thomas Photography.

Maggie Bergman, Wattle, 2005. Fine silver, leaded enamel. Photo by the artist.

Two clays, two peas

So many possibilities remain to be explored working with this fairly new medium of metal clay. It can be adapted for use with other media in ways that weren't possible in the past with traditional metalworking techniques. Several artists, including Noortje Meijerink and Alexandra Daini, create amazing work with metal clay and ceramics. This project uses low-fire ceramic clay and glazes to add tiny touches of color with great impact.

color

Medium/technique
Glazed ceramic clay

Tools & supplies
- Low-fire ceramic clay
- Low-fire underglazes: intense yellow, dark green, and light green
- Clear transparent glaze
- Craft sticks
- Small stiff-bristle paintbrush
- Plastic cup or wax paper
- Kiln paper

Metal clay
- 9 grams fine-silver clay

Metal clay toolkit (p. 7)

Additional tools & supplies
- Pair of earring wires

Success with ceramics

Metal clay and ceramic artists use very similar tools. The most important common tool, of course, is the kiln. By using low-fire pottery clay and glazes, small ceramics can be fired at temperatures suited to our metal clay kilns.

The ceramic elements that I incorporate into metal clay jewelry are very small, and thus the firing and cooling times are shorter than the traditional schedule. By working small, I reduce the chances of temperature shock and stress-related issues due to shrinkage in the clay and glaze. Low-fire ceramic clay and glazes are designed to be compatible with each other, and low-fire glazes flow at a temperature slightly higher than the sintering temperature of metal clay.

Pottery glaze is basically a glass coating over a fired clay body. Metal clay has been successfully fired onto lampworked beads and fused glass, so it's logical that metal clay can also be fired onto glazed ceramic using the same techniques.

Glass is colored using metal oxides, and achieving color is more difficult than just mixing pigments. Silver is one of the oxides used to color glass. Because of this, some oxides in the glaze react with the silver. To avoid this, I use underglaze to add the color with a clear-glaze top coat. Only the clear glaze comes into contact with the silver, and I avoid unpredictable metal oxide reactions.

Keep the ceramic elements small and use low-fire clay, underglazes, and a low-fire clear glaze. You will keep the clay goddesses happy and have a successful project!

Prepare the ceramic components

Pinch off a piece of low-fire pottery clay and roll it into a small ball approximately ⁵⁄₁₆" (8mm) in diameter. Repeat to make a total of four balls. Set the balls aside to dry **[A]**. Drying time could be as much as several hours. You can speed up the drying process by placing the balls on top of a warm kiln.

> Don't use a dehydrator; it will aggressively dry and shrink the surface of the ball while the interior remains wet, which could cause the surface to crack.

When the balls are totally dry, apply the underglaze: Open the jar of intense yellow underglaze and stir it well with a craft stick. The glaze should be the consistency of heavy cream. Mix distilled water into the glaze if it is too thick. Brush the underglaze onto the balls, being sure to cover the entire surface **[B]**. Set the balls aside to dry. From this point on, always set the balls bottom down on your work surface. This will keep the top of the ball, which is not going to be covered by metal clay, nice and smooth.

Open the jars of dark and light green underglaze and stir them to the right consistency. Dip a small stiff-bristle brush in the dark green glaze and dab the brush onto a paper towel until it's almost dry. Using the brush and a pouncing motion, apply the glaze lightly onto the ball. The dark green glaze should resemble small dots, not brushstrokes. Apply lightly; use just enough of the dark green to show a little color. Repeat using the light green. You can use your fingers to blend slightly by rolling the clay ball between your fingers **[C]**. Set aside to dry, bottom down.

When the underglaze is dry, move the balls to a kiln shelf and place the shelf in the kiln. Program the kiln to full ramp to 1920°F (1049°C) and hold for 15 minutes. Do not open the kiln until the temperature is under 200°F (93°C). Allow the balls to cool to room temperature.

Shake and stir the container of low-fire clear transparent gloss glaze to make sure it is mixed completely. Put a few large drops of glaze in a cup or on wax paper. Place a ceramic ball into the glaze. Roll the ball in the glaze until it is totally covered **[D]**. Use tweezers to transfer the ball, bottom down, to a sheet of paper to dry. Repeat to coat the remaining balls with clear gloss glaze.

Place a sheet of kiln paper on a kiln shelf. When the balls are completely dry, place them on the shelf paper with enough space

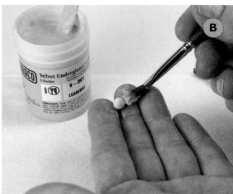

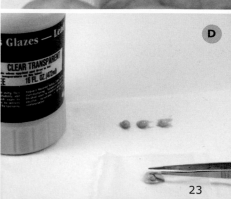

between them so they don't touch **[E]**. Place the shelf in the kiln. Fire again using the same firing schedule program as before: full ramp to 1920°F (1049°C), hold for 15 minutes, and then off. Again, do not open the kiln until the internal temperature is under 200°F (93°C).

Combine the ceramic balls with metal clay

Roll all of the metal clay on a texture sheet to 4 cards/1mm thick. I like to work thick because the clay will shrink and lock around the ceramic element; if the clay is thin, it will tear as it shrinks. Use a circle cutter or template and a needle tool to cut a ⅞" (22mm) diameter circle.

Slightly fold the wet clay circle in half. Do not crease it; just make a depression where you can place the ceramic balls. Add a little metal clay slip at the fold and place the clay balls bottom down in the fold **[F]**. Dampen the edges of the circle and pinch the edges closed above and below the ceramic balls. Gently push the edges in slightly around the balls **[G]**.

With a needle tool, make a hole at one end where the earring wire will go. Set aside to dry. Repeat to make the second peas-and-pod assembly.

Nestle the pods in vermiculite in a shallow firing container (I used a stainless steel pan) on a kiln shelf **[H]**. Fire to 1470°F (799°C) and hold for 30 minutes. Allow the kiln to cool completely to room temperature before opening the kiln door.

Finish the earrings

Finish the earrings any way you like. I prefer the look of a dark, liver of sulfur patina against the bright colors of the ceramic. Attach an earring wire to each pod.

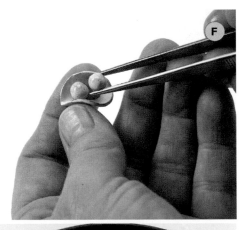

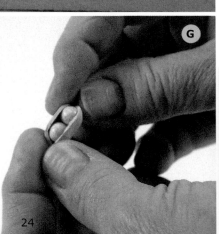

Ivy Solomon, Inside Branches, 2011. Sterling silver, fine silver, resin, 22k gold. Photo by Steve Solomon.

Hadar Jacobson, Butterfly, 2011. Copper, bronze, steel, white bronze. Photo by the artist.

Julia Rai, Treasures of the Deep, 2011. Fine silver, glass paints, Gilders paste, ceramic paint. Photo by Paul Mounsey.

Lorena Angulo, Calavera Mariposa, 2010. *Bronze, brass wire, gesso, acrylic paint. Photo by George Post.*

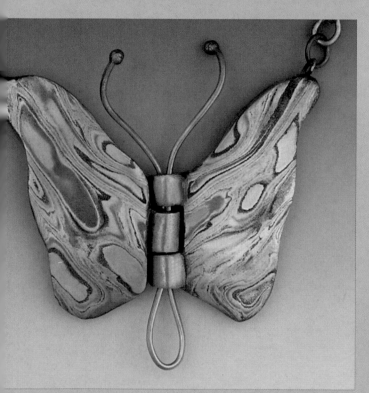

Wanaree Tanner, Fion McCumhil, 2011. *Copper, gesso, colored pencil, copper wire. Photo by the artist.*

Joy Funnell, Creative Mists, 2011. *Fine silver, enamel, lab-created green garnet. Photo by the artist.*

Flor earrings

The colorful flowers I saw as a kid growing up in small cities of Mexico are my inspiration for these earrings. I used Gilders paste, a durable wax medium available in a wide range of colors, to add bright highlights to bronze. The color brings good energy and happiness to those who wear this pair.

color

Medium/technique
Gilders paste

Supplies
• Gilders paste: Tulip Red, African Bronze, white
• Mineral spirits
• Clear spray lacquer (such as Permalac)

Metal clay
• 25 grams bronze clay

Metal clay toolkit (p. 7)

Additional tools & supplies
• 2 embeddable bronze eyelets
• Pair of earring wires
• 2 5mm freshwater pearls
• 2 headpins

Make the metal clay branches

Roll a clay cylinder about 5" (13cm) long and ⅛" (3mm) thick **[A]**. Cut the cylinder in half to create two 2½" (64mm) cylinders that will form the center of each earring's branch.

Form a loop at the end of each cylinder and add water to the joins of the loop and the whole cylinder to prevent it from drying **[B]**. Be sure to keep the clay moist as you work. Roll another 2½" (64mm) cylinder and cut it in half to form the cross-section of the branch. Add some water before adding this new piece to the center branch. Use a clay shaper to gently press the cross-section down in the center where it contacts the center branch **[C]**. Be careful to not break the shape. Let the branches dry.

Fill the backs of the branches with more fresh clay, paying extra attention to the join on the back of the two branches **[D]**. Add water in the area before adding some fresh clay, and smooth with a clay shaper. Let the branches dry.

Shape the leaves

Hand-sculpt a little teardrop shape and press with your fingers to flatten it very slightly **[E]**. Using the needle tool, mark veins on the leaf, pressing the tool gently into the clay **[F]**.

Apply water to the top of the branch where you will place a leaf. Position the leaf and press down gently with your fingers. Smooth the clay on the bottom of the leaf to join it to the branch using a clay shaper **[G]**. Repeat to make three leaves for each earring. Let the pieces dry.

With a craft knife, carve the back of the branches where they are connected to the leaves. This will create a finished look on the back **[H]**. Carve only some of the higher areas of the branch to make the connection with the leaf more natural looking.

Texture the surface

Add texture to the branches with a needle tool on both sides of the earring **[I]**. Use a light touch; just move the tool gently up and down in different directions. This will create a very organic look.

Use a fine-tip brush to add water to the bottom of the front of a leaf. Roll a small ball of fresh clay, gently press it onto a leaf, and

A note about size

Following the instructions, these earrings will be about 2" (51mm) long without the earring wires. If you want smaller earrings, make the cylinders more slender and form shorter branches.

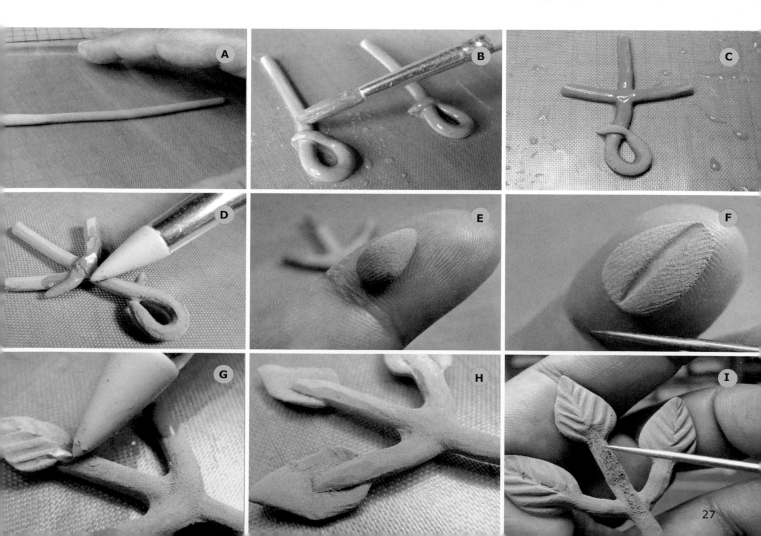

add a bit more water to the ball. Repeat to add a ball to each leaf [J].

Make the flowers
Roll about 10 grams of clay to 3 cards/.75mm thick. Use a needle tool to cut two flowers to fit the center of each branch [K]. Pick up the flowers and let them dry on the tip of the small brush, molding them a little to create a cupped form.

With a needle tool, make some lines on each petal of the dry flowers. Apply water to the back of the flower and to the area on the branch where you will place the flower. Press a small ball of fresh clay into the wet area on the branch. Use a fine-tip brush to press the flower over the fresh ball of clay [L]. Turn the branch over and smooth the fresh clay that spread as you pressed. Repeat for the second earring. Let the pieces dry.

Make a small rosebud with a little piece of fresh clay. With the needle tool, apply the rosebud to the center of each flower [M]. Gently press the rosebud down and add water. Let the piece air-dry.

Embed the brass eyelet in a small ball of fresh clay and place the ball on the back of the center leaf. Using a clay shaper, smooth the clay on the sides only [N]. Add water and let it dry. Repeat for the second earring.

Fire the earrings according to the metal clay manufacturer's instructions. Let the earrings cool. Finish the metal by burnishing them with a brass brush in soapy water and putting them in a tumbler for at least 30 minutes.

A single component makes a lovely pendant. Make your own beaded chain with bronze wire and beads.

Apply the Gilders paste
Using a few drops of mineral spirits, dilute some African Bronze paste to a creamy consistency and apply to the leaves using a small brush [O]. Repeat with white paste to cover the whole flower except the rosebud [P]. Let the white dry a little in the flower before you apply the final color, Tulip Red, over the white [Q]. Let the earrings dry for at least 12 hours. Seal the colors with a thin coat of clear lacquer. Dry for 2–4 hours and attach earring wires and a bead dangle if desired.

Golden arrows

One of my passions is carving wax models for lost wax casting. Carving in dry metal clay is just as rewarding to me, but with a bonus: I can have a completed piece within a few hours rather than days. I landed on this color technique after seeing a video of someone using alcohol ink to color lunch boxes. In this project, I layer color over lovely carved texture.

color

Medium/technique
Alcohol ink

Tools & supplies
• Alcohol ink
• Alcohol blending solution
• Watercolor paint palette
• Sable hair paintbrush #00
  (for ink)
• Cotton swabs
• Craft brush (for water)
• Decoupage medium

Metal clay
- 16 grams fine-silver clay
- Paste clay
- Syringe clay

Metal clay toolkit (p. 7)

Additional tools & supplies
- Triangle template
- 5" (13cm) of 20-gauge fine-silver wire
- Masking tape
- Pointed brass millimeter (mm) calipers
- Masking tape
- Carving tool
- Wire cutters
- Large bail-making pliers or ⅜" (9mm) diameter wooden dowel
- Flatnose pliers
- Stainless steel scraper
- Lavender oil
- Jewelers Black or liver of sulfur
- Natural bristle brush for the Jewelers Black
- 2 4mm black onyx beads
- Cup bur for 20-gauge wire

Make your own carving tool

Retired dental implements make great carving tools. Using a jeweler's saw and a 4/0 blade, saw off the tip of the dental tool at the point where it bends downward. File the end to a taper. If filed correctly, the tool will cut a small groove when you pull it across dry clay.

Preserving the color

I was curious about how durable this color treatment was, so I started to experiment. I found that alcohol ink color performed very much like a patina achieved via liver of sulfur. I painted the ink on a fired piece with texture and smooth highlights, and tumbled it with stainless steel shot for 30 minutes. The ink was removed from the high spots, but stayed in the recesses—much like a liver of sulfur patina. I tried scratching the ink on the surface of the metal to see if it would flake off. It did not. But just as a black patina can be scratched through, so can the ink. I heated the inked metal with a torch and found just as liver of sulfur patina burns off, so will the ink. The down side to the ink is its solvent, alcohol. If it is soaked in alcohol or rubbed with an alcohol-treated cloth, the alcohol ink dissolves.

I tested different additives to protect the ink. Lacquer or Permalac are solvent-based, and thus they dissolve the ink. Renaissance wax does not protect the ink. A fast-drying polyurethane sealed the ink well but yellowed over time. Mod Podge, a water-based decoupage product, works well if thinned with water. If applied thick, it can peel off.

Prepare the earring wires
Cut the fine-silver wire into two 2½" (64mm) pieces. Make indentions on the last ³⁄₁₆" (5mm) of each wire using wire cutters (be careful not to cut through the wire). Bend the textured end of each wire to a 45-degree angle using flatnose pliers.

Create the silver clay earring bases
Roll the lump clay to 5 cards/1.25mm thick. Using a needle tool and the plastic template (or the template provided), cut two 1³⁄₁₆" (21mm) wide triangle shapes **[A]**. Transfer

the triangles to a stainless steel scraper. Make an imprint of each wire end into the top of both clay pieces by pressing the bent wire ends halfway into the wet clay and then removing them **[B]**. Place the scraper, with the clay, onto a mug warmer.

Warming the clay components on a scraper allows them to dry without warping.

Refine the bases and carve a groove
Smooth the back, sides, and top of both

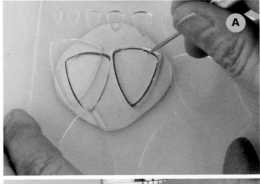

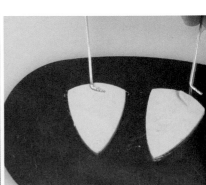

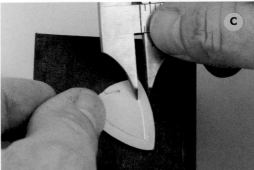

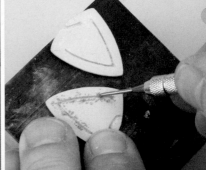

earrings using coarse and then fine emery boards. Set the brass calipers to 3mm and lock them with a piece of masking tape.

On the top and bottom of the calipers, you'll see a vertical line (I darkened the line with permanent marker). As you slide the caliper jaws open, align this mark at the measurement you want; millimeters (mm) are at the bottom and inches are at the top.

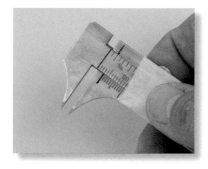

Place one earring base on a rubber block. Place the back caliper tip on the side of the clay and the front tip on the top. Drag the calipers around the bottom V-shape area while lightly pressing into the top of the clay so the front tip carves a line into the clay **[C]**. Carving lightly several times works best. Repeat the process until the line is well drawn. Now make the line deeper by dragging the carving tool along the line with a pulling action **[D]**. Use a craft knife to scribe an accent line at the base of the

earring. Deepen the line using the edge of a triangular needle file **[E]**. Repeat with the other earring base.

Carve the center texture
Set the brass calipers to 2mm and lock them with a piece of masking tape. Starting at the base of the V in the interior shape of the earrings, lightly mark points along the carved groove all the way to the top (see **template**). Place the back caliper tip on the junction of the accent line and the outline **[F]**. Apply pressure to the front tip, making a small mark. Place the back tip of the calipers onto the new mark. Apply pressure to the front tip, making another small mark **[G]**. Repeat until you have made eight evenly spaced marks, and then repeat to make marks along the other side of the earring base using the same process.

Use a pencil to draw lines from point to point, following the template. If needed, sand with fine sandpaper to erase mistakes. Using a pulling action with the dental tool, carve lightly along each line. Repeat the process to carve the lines deeper **[H]**.

Create the top earring layer
Roll clay to 6 cards/1.5mm thick. Using the same template you used previously, cut one triangle of clay. Remove the excess clay around the shape. Place a bowed tissue blade 4mm down from the top and

template (actual size)

cut the shape into two pieces **[I]**. Transfer the pieces to the stainless steel scraper and place on a mug warmer until semidry. Repeat to make a second top layer for the other earring. Don't dry these top layers completely so they'll be flexible enough to press over the earring wires.

Attach the top layer to bottom layer
Create oil paste by mixing 3–5 drops of lavender oil into the paste clay. Paint the textured end of the wire with the oil paste. Place the wire into the impression on the bottom piece. Paint oil paste over the wire and the clay where the top layer will attach **[J]**. Paint oil paste onto the back of the top layer. While the top earring layer is semidry, attach it to the bottom layer, sandwiching the bent wire tip between the layers. Make sure the end of the wire does not extend below the top layer. Press the two layers together and hold for 30 seconds or until there is no movement after you release pressure. Place on the mug warmer and dry completely.

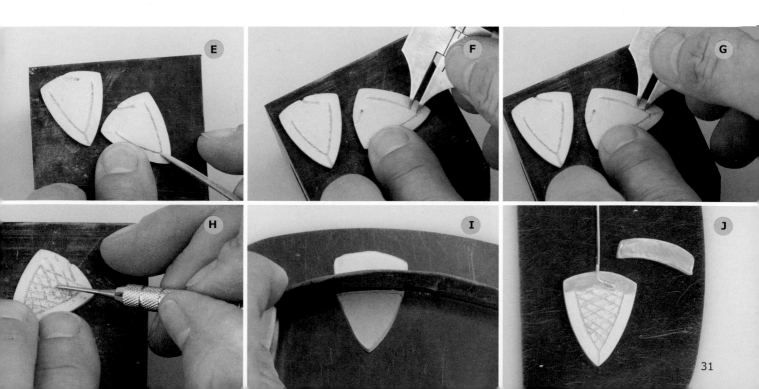

Tips for using alcohol ink

A plastic watercolor palette is handy for working with and storing alcohol ink. Place 5–6 drops of alcohol ink into each well and label it. The ink dries within minutes; reactivate it by adding a few drops of blending solution. Use a fine-tip natural-bristle brush to apply the ink to the metal. I keep one brush for each color and label it with the ink's name; this way I don't have to clean the brush between colors. The dried ink makes the brush stiff, but dipping it into the solvent on the palette reactivates the ink and softens the brush. Use the ink as if it were watercolor paint. The more blending solution you add, the lighter the ink color. The colors mix well while liquid, so it's easy to add more colors to the palette if you like. Painting the ink in layers creates a painterly texture. To keep debris out of the tray between uses, store the palette in a plastic bag.

I burnish the metal by tumbling it to compress the pores of the fired metal clay. This improves the application of the ink. For trouble spots, I burnish the carved areas or apply a watered-down base coat of decoupage medium. Allow the coating to dry fully before applying ink.

Check the join around the wire and between the two pieces. If you find gaps between the layers, spackle lump clay into the gaps by wetting the clay with a wet brush, picking up a small bit of lump clay using a flat clay shaper, and then pressing the clay into the gaps **[K]**. If necessary, reinforce around the wire with syringe clay and dry again.

Refine the dry clay earrings, file the top ornament, and fire

Smooth the edges on both earrings using a fine-grit emery board. Round the bottom layer's sides from the groove to the edge by filing with the emery board **[L]**. Do not hold the piece by the wire; it may pull out. If this happens, paint the hole with oil paste and reinsert the wire into the piece.

Draw two pencil lines as shown on the top layer **[M]**. File a groove along the pencil lines using the edge of a triangle needle file. Use a coarse file to taper the sides, leaving the center high **[N]**. Use fine-grit sanding pads

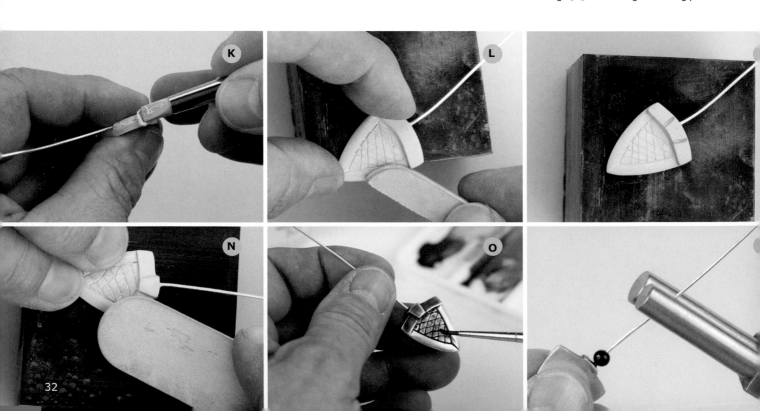

to remove deep scratches from all of the surfaces. Repeat for the other earring. Fire both pieces in a kiln according to the metal clay manufacturer's instructions.

Finish and add color to the earrings

Burnish the metal by scrubbing with soapy water and a brass brush or tumbling them for 10 minutes in a rotary tumbler with stainless steel shot and burnishing solution. Use a burnisher to burnish the carved indentions. Apply Jewelers Black or liver of sulfur solution with a natural-bristle brush to the carved area.

Remove the patina on the raised areas using polishing sponges. Place 5–6 drops of alcohol ink in a well of the watercolor palette, add two drops of blending solution, and paint the ink onto the textured areas [O]. Apply two coats, making it darker in certain areas as desired. When the ink is dry, seal the fronts of the earrings with decoupage medium. Allow it to dry. Slide a 4mm onyx bead onto each earring wire, placing it next to the top of the earring.

Using the large bail-making pliers (or nylon-jaw pliers), work-harden the wire by pulling the wire through the lightly closed jaws [P] several times. Bend the wire around the large bail jaw, bending it into a curved earring wire. Bend the other earring at the same spot. Bend the ends of the wires outward using flatnose pliers and trim any excess using wire cutters. Twist a cup bur on the end of the wire to smooth it [Q].

Pam East, Blue Green Dreams, 2011. Fine silver, leaded enamel, pearl. Photo by the artist.

Louis Duhamel, Tiny Tunes, 2009. Fine silver, sterling silver, paper, resin. Photo by the artist.

Q

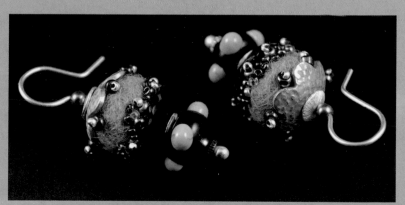

Barbara Briggs, Moss Plum Drops, 2010. Bronze, fine silver, sterling silver, felt, seed beads, Lucite, brass, lampworked glass beads. Photo by the artist.

DESIGNER **Lorena Angulo**

Mi corazón

Corazones (hearts) are a motif I have always been passionate about. I look to my Mexican heritage and culture for inspiration, and this pendant is my interpretation of a sacred heart milagro. My technique of coloring a base of paper clay produces a substantial but surprisingly lightweight pendant. To me, this sculpted heart pendant symbolizes many things: love, certainly, but also our passion for what we do in life, health, compassion, and friendship.

 color

Medium/technique
Colored pencil over paper clay

Tools & supplies
• Creative Paperclay
• Colored pencils
• Fixative
• Clear lacquer

Metal clay
• 25 grams bronze clay

Metal clay toolkit (p. 7)

Additional tools & supplies
• Linoleum cutter with V-tip gouge
• Two-part epoxy

template (actual size)

Make the metal clay frame

Draw a framed heart pattern on paper. You can use the **template** provided or create your own design. Roll a sheet of metal clay about 3 cards/.75mm thick and place the stencil on top. Using a needle tool, cut the outline from the clay **[A]**. Remove the stencil and let the clay dry.

Using a pencil, draw the heart shape and additional details as desired on the clay. Using a linoleum cutter with a V-tip gouge, gently carve along the pencil lines **[B]**. Be careful to not break the piece; the clay is very porous and it carves very easily. If you'd like holes in the frame, use a craft knife: Twist the knife at the points you'd like holes until the holes are the size you want **[C]**. Carve some lines to add detail to the border around the heart **[D]**.

Make the bezel

Roll a sheet of metal clay about 4 cards/1mm thick, ¼" (7mm) wide, and about 4" (10cm) long. This strip will become the bezel around the heart. Dampen the outline of the heart and shape the strip on its edge over the outline, placing the seam top and center. Place the piece on a mug warmer. Working on the warmer, continue adjusting the bezel until it is dry enough to hold its shape. Remove it from the mug warmer. Apply more water **[E]** and be sure the bezel is in full contact with the heart base.

On the inside of the heart, moisten the seam of the bezel and add a little fresh clay. Smooth the fresh clay with a clay shaper **[F]**. Add more water at the outside of the seam to secure it **[G]**. Let the piece dry again.

Roll a clay cylinder 1½" (38mm) long and ⁵⁄₃₂" (4mm) thick to make the bail for the pendant. Spiral one end, add water, loosely curve the other end, and trim the end. Let the shape dry **[H]**.

Add water to the point on the back of the frame where the top of the bail will attach. Place a little ball of fresh clay in the spot and press the bail in place. Use a clay shaper to smooth the fresh clay **[I]**. Finish by adding a little more water. Let the frame and bail dry completely. Fire according to the clay manufacturer's instructions.

After the piece cools, burnish it with a brass brush and soapy water. Place it in a rotary tumbler with steel shot and burnishing compound for at least 30 minutes.

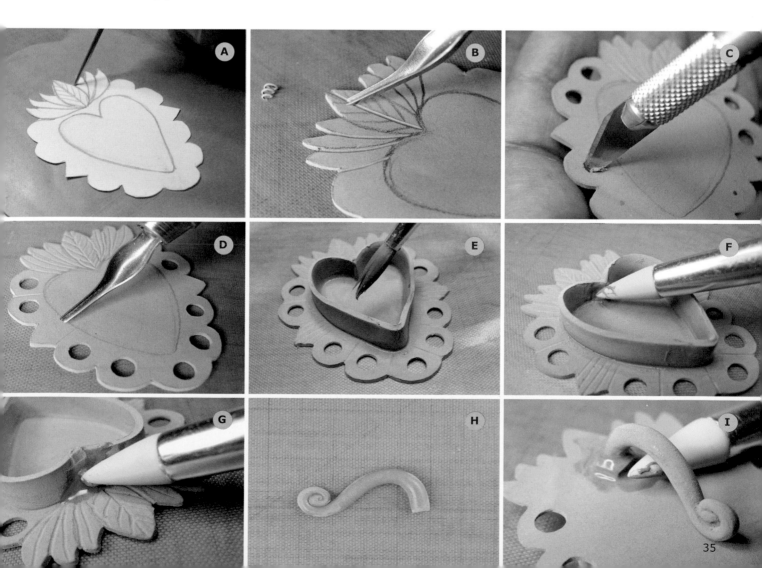

Shape the paper clay heart cabochon

Overfill the bezel interior with paper clay and let the clay dry [J]. When it's dry to the touch (a fingernail doesn't leave a mark), take it out of the bezel and let the cabochon dry fully.

The cabochon will take 2–3 days to dry fully at room temperature. The drying time on a mug warmer is considerably shorter: a few hours. The cabochon may shrink slightly as it dries.

When the cabochon is totally dry, use your fingers to apply a bit of water and fresh paper clay to fill any cracks that developed. Let the cabochon dry again on a mug warmer for an hour. After the cabochon is dry, test the fit by inserting it inside the bezel. Use a craft knife to trim excess paper clay until the cabochon fits properly. Sand the cabochon smooth with 1000-grit sand paper [K]. Use the carving tool to carve a design in the surface of the cabochon [L].

Add color

Color the cabochon as desired with colored pencil. The carved lines will appear white when the first layer of colored pencil is applied [M]. Apply several layers of color for best results. Add fixative to seal the first color. Choose a second color of pencil to fill the carved lines, sharpen it to a very fine point, and color the carved lines.

Seal the cabochon with a clear lacquer. Let the varnish dry [N]. Use two-part epoxy to glue the paper clay cabochon inside the bezel and let the epoxy dry completely.

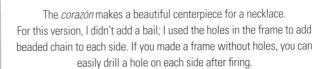

The *corazón* makes a beautiful centerpiece for a necklace. For this version, I didn't add a bail; I used the holes in the frame to add beaded chain to each side. If you made a frame without holes, you can easily drill a hole on each side after firing.

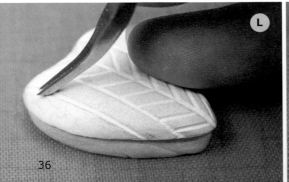

Mokume gane daisy

Various types of metal clay can be mixed into lovely, organic patterns reminiscent of mokume gane in traditional metalwork. Using Baldwin's patina enhances the contrast between the metals. I used my own powdered metal clay in this project; you can find more information on the clay as well as firing instructions that apply to most brands on my blog (see Sources and Resources, p. 111).

color

Medium/technique
Mokume gane with varied metal clay types, enhanced with patina

Tools & supplies
• Baldwin's patina

Metal clay
• Quick-fire powder-form clay: copper (25 grams), bronze (12 grams), white bronze (12 grams), and steel clay (either kind, 6 grams)

Metal clay toolkit (p. 7)

Additional tools & supplies
• Clay extruder
• 20- or 18-gauge bronze wire eyelets (or embeddable loop findings)
• Slender straw
• Rotary tool or flex shaft
• Slotted mandrel
• Soft matting wheel or extra-fine steel wool
• 120-grit sanding drum (optional)

Make a cane for the petals

Roll four sheets of metal clay: copper to 6 cards/1.5mm thick; bronze to 3 cards/.75mm; steel to 1 card/.25mm; and white bronze to 3 cards/.75mm. Use the barrel end of the clay extruder to cut six disks out of each clay layer **[A]**.

Stack the disks, alternating them in the following order: copper, bronze, steel, and white bronze. Insert the stack into the extruder. Insert a copper disk with a 6mm hole of any shape at the extruder's opening **[B]**. Extrude the whole stack **[C]**. Cut the extruded cane into four equal lengths. Stack the canes side by side **[D]** and roll them into a tight cylinder. As you roll, the cylinder

will lengthen. Press with your fingers from both ends until it is shortened to its original length **[E]**. Twist the ends of the cane in opposite directions **[F]**. Roll the cane back into a cylinder shape **[G]**. Make sure it stays at its original length.

Shape the cylinder into a triangular cane **[H]**. Using a scraper or a tissue blade, slice five segments from the cane **[I]**.

> For clean cuts, refrigerate the cane for about 15 minutes or let the cane dry halfway before slicing.

Roll a clay base and assemble the flower

Roll a layer of copper clay 3 cards/.75mm

thick. Wet it, and lay the triangles on the sheet in the pattern of a flower **[J]**. Cut away the excess sheet around the flower **[K]**. Embed a wire eyelet made from 20- or 18-gauge bronze wire into the petal next to the top center petal **[L]**. Repeat on the other side. Using a straw, cut a circle in the middle of the flower **[M]**. Dry the flower thoroughly.

Fill the gaps between the copper base and each flower petal with copper clay. Fill the gaps around the eyelets with copper clay as well. Dry the flower again.

Sand the front, sides, and back of the flower smooth with a fine (150-grit) sanding sponge

Vickie Hallmark, Perched, 2010.
Fine silver, copper, torch-fired enamel, fine-silver wire. Photo by the artist.

[N]. Make a little ball out of white bronze clay and insert it in the center hole **[O]**. Dry again. Burnish the surface of the flower **[P]**. This will help minimize gaps caused by the different shrinkage rates of the clays.

Fire and finish
Fire the flower following the clay manufacturer's instructions.

Following the two-phase firing schedule is highly recommended. Since the flower is big and contains a lot of binder to burned away, fire for 2 hours at the first phase. Stove-top firing is recommended for this phase.

If the surface of the flower is uneven despite the burnishing, sand it flush with a 120-grit sanding drum. Sand all surfaces smooth with 220-grit sandpaper. Move on to 400 grit. I like to wrap sandpaper around a slotted mandrel in a rotary tool to get at the center and sides of the piece.

Matte the surface with extra-fine steel wool or a soft matting fiber wheel on the rotary tool. To highlight the contrast between the metals, use a cotton swab to apply a little bit of Baldwin's patina to the surface. Wash it off right away and let it air-dry.

Janet Alexander, Summer Fun, 2011.
Fine silver, alcohol ink. Photo by Marsha Thomas Photography.

Pam East, Sunflower, 2011.
Fine silver, leaded enamel. Photo by the artist.

Polymer petals

Intricate polymer canework and the beautiful gradients of a Skinner blend are perfect counterparts to silver clay that gets its warm-toned patina from liver of sulfur. Layering these elements creates visual depth and a richness of texture not possible with either medium alone. In-depth instructions for a variety of blends and canework are easy to find in books and other sources; choose your favorites for the centerpiece flower and the other beads in the necklace.

color

Medium/technique
Polymer clay

Tools & supplies
- 2 2-oz. blocks of polymer clay in 3 colors of your choice
- Translucent liquid polymer clay
- Oven for baking the polymer clay
- Pasta machine for making the Skinner blend
- Clear glass microbeads
- 11º seed beads in colors of your choice
- Accent and filler beads of your choice
- Fireline or Wildfire beading thread
- #12 beading needle
- Large-hole crimps

Metal clay
- 50 grams fine-silver clay

Metal clay toolkit (p. 7)

Additional tools & supplies
- Flower templates
- Beading awl
- Leaves, twigs, or other texturing items
- Cold-molding silicone putty
- Cooking spray
- Chasing hammer
- Dapping block and punches
- 24" (61cm) 20-gauge fine-silver wire
- Flush wire cutters
- Flatnose pliers
- Stepped forming pliers
- 2 fine-silver eyepins or 2 screw eyes
- .015 flexible beading wire
- Large-hole wire guard
- Clasp

Make the metal clay flowers

To make the metal clay flowers, create your own template or use a purchased cutter. I made negative-space templates of flower shapes in four graduated sizes [A].

Roll the metal clay to 4 cards/1mm thick. To texture the clay, I used a real leaf with prominent veining on the underside; you can also draw the veins with an awl or hatpin. Center the largest template over the clay and firmly press the lightly oiled back of the leaf into the clay with your finger [B].

Use a craft knife to cut out the flower shape following the template. Make a hole in the center large enough to accommodate 20-gauge wire. For my necklace, I repeated this process to make a total of one large, two medium, two small, and two extra-small flowers. Let your flowers dry completely. Smooth any rough edges with emery boards or sanding pads.

Shape the twigs

I made molds of real twigs using cold-molding silicone putty following the manufacturer's instructions. It's best to use twigs that are fairly straight and without projections that might cause an undercut. Spray the twig mold with anti-stick cooking spray and wipe off the excess before carefully pushing the metal clay into the mold. Smooth the top of the metal clay with a moist finger. When dry, pop the metal clay twig out of the mold. Push a fine-silver eyepin or screw eye into the top of each twig. (You also can solder on a jump ring after the twigs are fired.) Carefully clean up any rough edges with a moist finger or files [C].

Fire the metal clay components

Place the dry metal clay flowers and twigs on a kiln shelf and place this in the kiln. Fire according to the metal clay manufacturer's instructions.

Finish

After the pieces are cool, brush them with a brass brush and water. Keep the centerpiece flower flat and make the other flower shapes into domed shapes using a dapping block and large dap [D]. Dap the two smallest flowers to face up and the four remaining flowers to face down.

Cut five 4" (10cm) pieces of 20-gauge fine-silver wire. Flux the wires and ball the ends using a torch. (You can use long headpins instead, if you like.)

Another technique is to make your own headpins by forming a bit of metal clay into a ball and sliding the wire into the ball. Fire these headpins along with the other metal clay components. After firing and cooling, brush these balled-end wires with a brass brush and water.

Layer the domed flowers as shown and insert the balled-end wire through the layers [E]. Using stepped forming pliers, create a coil below the layered flowers [F]. Use a palette knife to pry the coil slightly apart in the middle [G]. The two coils will each hold a strand of beading wire as you string the necklace.

Grasp each half of the coil with flatnose pliers and spread them to create two perpendicular coils [H]. (The centerpiece flower coil will be completed later, after the polymer clay is set onto it.)

Tumble the metal pieces in a rotary tumbler with steel shot, water and a liquid burnishing compound for 15–30 minutes. Check if you are satisfied with the sheen; tumble longer if needed. Be careful not to remove texture by tumbling too long.

Make the polymer clay canes
Create several coordinating canes in polymer clay. You'll use these canes for the centerpiece and also for the beads in the remainder of the necklace. For my centerpiece, I made four sheets of a Skinner blend using red, gold, and translucent colors of clay [I]. Each sheet was about the size of a standard postcard and had slight variations in color and color placement to create striations in the petals.

I like to layer a thin sheet of translucent clay between each Skinner blend sheet. Stack the sheets and compress the stack until it is about half its original size. Cut the stack in half, restack the two halves, and reduce further into an oval cane or as desired. (Various sizes of this cane can be used.) Use slices from the ends of this cane where interesting striations appear to make pod-shaped beads for the centerpiece and as accents [J].

Shape the polymer beads
You can create any variety of accent beads that you like. My necklace uses 18 round beads that are ½" (13mm) in diameter. Eight of the round beads are covered with cane slices. I also made 10 solid-color beads, coated them with liquid translucent polymer, and rolled them in glass microbeads to add texture.

The necklace also has seven pod-shaped beads made from the Skinner blend sheets. I inserted 1" (26mm) of wire into three of the beads so I could create bead dangles [K, inset]. For the centerpiece, make four pod-shaped beads that fit within the metal petals, exposing at least ⅛" (3mm) of metal. Shape the base beads out of scrap polymer clay and then apply very thin slices of cane around the base beads [K]. Carefully roll the beads in your hands until the cane slices have blended into the base bead. If you plan to add seed bead fringe, as I did, make the stringing hole in your polymer beads large enough to accommodate two strands of beading wire and several passes of thread.

Build the centerpiece
Apply a thin film of translucent liquid polymer to the surface of the metal clay flower centerpiece. Avoid covering the outer margin of metal that will show. Use a clay shaper to push the liquid polymer into all the grooves of the metal petals. Apply liquid polymer to the base of a polymer pod. Place the polymer pod on the metal petal and apply pressure until the two shapes contact tightly. Clean away any liquid polymer that seeps out. Repeat to add a total of four polymer pods to the metal clay centerpiece [L].

Bake the components
In a craft oven, bake the polymer clay beads and polymer/metal clay components according to the polymer clay manufacturer's instructions. Remove from oven when baked and let cool. Insert the remaining balled-end wire through the centerpiece, coil the wire on the forming pliers, and separate the two halves of the coil.

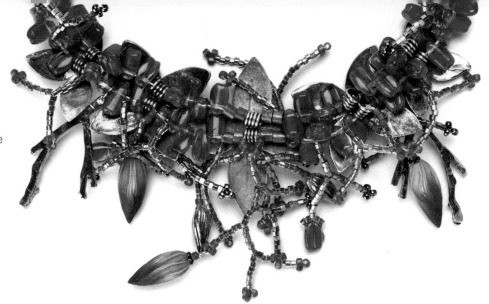

I strung accent beads and stitched free-form seed bead fringe behind the flower components.

Add patina

Achieving the desired color of patina on the metal can be tricky and unpredictable. For fine silver, I usually start with a very weak solution—a pea-size chunk of liver of sulfur in a cup of water. Have a bowl of water and a bit of baking soda solution nearby. Paint the liver of sulfur solution on the metal [M]. Rinse the component in the water to stop the color development. Keep repeating this process until you like the color, and then scrub it with baking soda solution and rinse.

String the necklace

Cut two 28" (71cm) pieces of beading wire. Treating the two wires as one, string half of the polymer beads on the wire. Separate the wires and string a seed bead on each strand. From this point, string accent beads on each wire separately as desired, interspersing flower and twig components. Pass only one strand of beading wire through each of the coils on the back of the metal clay flowers [N]. For the remaining half of the necklace, treat the two wires as

one and string a mirror-image pattern of the first half. Add crimp beads or tubes over the two strands of beading wire on each end. On each end, string a large-hole wire guard over the beading wire, pass the wire back into the crimp, and secure the crimp. Attach a closure of your choice.

Add fringe

To add fringe, thread 2 yd. (1.8m) of Fireline on a beading needle. Pick up a seed bead and sew through the seed bead several times to secure the thread. Sew through all the polymer beads, the remaining strand of the necklace, and the bottom row of coils until you reach the centerpiece. Sew through the lower coil of the centerpiece and pick up about six seed beads. Sew through the coil again and back through three of the seed beads. Pick up about 3" (76mm) of seed beads (or whatever length you like). You'll build on this length with branches of free-form fringe by passing through seed beads as shown [figure]. Continue to add fringe randomly

to fill, varying the lengths of the branches. Complete the fringe on half of the necklace, pass the needle through beads to return to the point where you began, and repeat on the other half of the necklace.

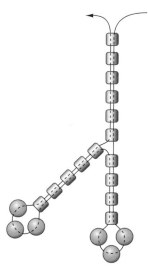

figure

DESIGNER **Joy Funnell**

Luminosity

I applied enamel into cells created with a texture plate and applied a liver of sulfur patina to create a glowing pendant. Extra texture comes from spirals shaped from fine-silver wire. I like to be sure the back of a piece is nearly as interesting as the front, so I incorporated a handmade texture and sparkling stones on the reverse.

color

Medium/technique
Enamel, patina, and fireable cubic zirconias (CZs)

Tools & supplies
- Enamels: Cattleya Lemon Yellow Middle S351, Toho Transparent Red DST-25
- Fireable CZs: 3mm yellow, 2mm light orange, 2mm dark orange
- Mortar and pestle
- Small, clean cups for the ground enamel
- Fine-tip paintbrush for enamel
- Paper towels

Metal clay
- 20 grams fine-silver clay
- Syringe clay
- Art Clay Silver Overlay Paste

Metal clay toolkit (p. 7)

Additional tools & supplies
- 12" (31 cm) 24-gauge (0.4mm) soft fine-silver wire
- Household ammonia
- Artists watercolor paper, approx. 4" (10cm) square
- Ball-head embossing tools
- Starburst texture sheet
- 1½" (38mm) circle cutter or template
- Small diamond-shaped cutter
- Waterbrush pen
- Baby wipes
- Flush wire cutters
- Jewelry pliers (flatnose and roundnose)
- Jewelry polishing cloth

It's important to me that the back of my work is nearly as interesting as the front. This texture is the result of the embossed paper technique.

Joy's tips and tricks

- Keep the finished piece at least 5 cards (1.25mm) thick so no counter-enamel is needed.
- Paper and card textures absorb lubricant, so use a wet baby wipe to cover any exposed clay while you lubricate paper and card textures just before using.
- Frequently clean the tip of your water brush on a baby wipe when cleaning around the wires.
- Always ensure fired silver clay pieces are dried well before refiring. Trapped moisture in the fired silver can cause air bubbles to blow up.
- Allow the piece to cool naturally after firing. Do not quench, which opens the pores and can dull the enamel colors.
- After firing, check that all the wires are well attached before brushing the piece. If they are loose, add more overlay paste and refire.
- A magnetic pin tumbler provides a good finish for enamelling. Or brush the piece under water using a stainless steel brush and then burnish with an agate burnisher.
- Use transparent jewelry enamels rather than opaque to let the silver shine through.
- Use colors that do not need any clear flux underneath to get better depth of color in the two layers.

Prepare the enamels

Transparent jewelry enamels should be washed and ground before wet-packing into the metal recesses. This ensures the particles of enamel are a small, uniform size and impurities are washed away, which creates clear colors. When using opaque enamels, grinding is not so important; a rinse will suffice.

Place the enamel powder in a mortar and add some tap water. Use the pestle to grind the enamel until it feels less gritty and has a smoother sound to it, but do not grind so long that you end up with a very fine powder. Let the enamel settle and then carefully pour off the excess water. Add more water, let it settle again, and drain. Keep repeating until the drained water is clear. For best results, do the two final rinses in distilled or demineralized water. On the last rinse, leave a little water in the mortar, swirl it around with the enamel, and empty it into your small, clean pot so the enamel is covered by a thin layer of water.

Create the texture for the back

Using a ball-head embossing tool, draw a pattern onto a piece of watercolor paper. Use sufficient pressure to create an indented pattern **[A]**. To make the pattern more defined, go over the lines again.

Thanks to artist Lynne Glazzard for giving me the idea for this reusable embossed paper technique.

Lubricate the paper texture sheet and a second texture sheet (my sheet has a starburst pattern). Roll the silver clay to 7 cards/1.75mm thick. Place the clay on the starburst texture. Place 5-card/1.25mm thickness gauges on each side of the clay on top of the texture sheet. Place the paper texture face down on the clay with the gauges inside the texture sandwich **[B]**. Roll across in one firm smooth action. The clay is now textured on both sides.

Place the clay on the nonstick surface and use the circle cutter to cut a circle from the starburst pattern **[C]**.

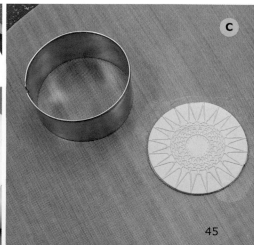

45

Use a diamond-shaped cutter to cut out evenly spaced V shapes all around the edge **[D]**. Dry the piece. Smooth the edges using a baby wipe wrapped around a cocktail stick to get into the recesses **[E]**.

Make a bail for the back

Roll a short cylinder of clay. Place 6-card thickness gauges on each side of the cylinder and roll it flat. Lay the clay onto the lubricated handmade paper texture with 4-card thickness gauges on each side on top of the texture. Roll again to texture the clay. Cut out a rectangle approximately 1¼ x ¼" (30 x 6mm) **[F]**. With the texture facing outward, wrap the rectangle of clay around a lubricated plastic straw in the shape of a question mark and allow to dry **[G]**. This will become the pendant bail.

Refine the edges of the bail using sandpaper **[H]** and use a baby wipe to smooth them. Allow the bail to dry. Use syringe clay to attach the bail to the back of the pendant **[I]**.

Create bezels for the CZs

Extrude a small ball of syringe clay onto the back of the piece. Use tweezers to set a CZ on the clay, culet (pointed side) down **[J]**. Using the tip of the tweezers, gently push the CZ into the clay so the girdle (widest part) of the CZ sinks below the line of the clay. The table (flat top) of the stone should be level with the top surface of the clay or slightly below it so the clay ball becomes a bezel around the CZ. Dry. Repeat twice to create a pleasing design with the three CZs **[K]**.

Ensure your piece is thoroughly dry before firing. For enameling, low-fire fine-silver clay needs a minimum firing of 20 minutes at 1472°F (800°C), which is longer than the manufacturer's instructions. Fire. Allow the piece to cool naturally; do not quench. Polish in a magnetic pin tumbler or with a stainless steel brush under running water followed by a burnisher or rotary tumbler to create a bright, shiny finish.

Add details with silver wire

Use fine-silver wire to make spiral decorations, starting with the center spiral: Use roundnose pliers to create a small, open loop. Holding the loop with flatnose pliers, gently coil the wire into an open spiral shape to fit the center of the pendant design. Trim with flush wire cutters. Make

four tiny spirals, starting them with fine-point tweezers instead of the roundnose pliers. Use flatnose pliers to coil them into tight spirals **[L]**. Anneal the wire shapes in a kiln at 1472°F (800°C) for 2 minutes. You can use a torch, but this gauge of wire melts very quickly, so take great care. Handle the cooled annealed wires carefully as they are very soft and will easily bend out of shape. Place the shapes on the base and press them down gently with your finger to ensure they have good contact with the surface.

Put a small amount of overlay paste in a wideneck container (such as a small plastic cup), adding just enough water to create a thick, creamy consistency. (If it is thin and runny, it will not hold well.)

Using tweezers, carefully pick up a spiral **[M]** and dip it so just the underside of the shape is coated with overlay paste. Position it quickly on the pendant before the paste starts to dry. Repeat to attach all the spirals; the dry paste will hold them in place for firing. Check for gaps under the spirals; use a fine-tip paintbrush to add a little more overlay paste if needed.

Use the waterbrush pen to carefully clean any excess overlay paste from around the spirals and off the surface of the spirals **[N]**. Dry completely. Fire for 3 minutes at 1472°F (800°C) to fuse the spirals to the base.

Allow to cool and check that the spirals are secure. Burnish lightly with an agate burnisher and ensure you have no sharp ends **[O]**. If any part of the wire is not attached properly, apply some overlay paste under the wire, refire, and burnish again.

Make sure the fired pendant is totally dry. Place the pendant in the kiln at 1472°F (800°C) for 2 minutes. This burns off the oils from the surface, which will allow water to sheet over the surface without puddling. This is very important when wet-packing enamels. Allow to cool and do not touch the surface.

Apply the enamel colors

Organize your workspace with a clean piece of paper towel, the pendant, the prepared enamel colors, a small cup of distilled water, and a clean fine-tip paintbrush. Level the pendant by placing a paintbrush underneath, opposite the bail. Tilt the enamel cup so some enamel is above the water line and some is below. With the paintbrush tip, pick up yellow enamel from just above the waterline and carefully

place it into the center cell in a thin, even layer around and through the spiral **[P]** . If the enamel does not move around on the surface easily, add some wetter enamel.

Tap the side of the piece with the paintbrush handle to distribute the enamel grains evenly. Carefully remove excess moisture by touching a clean paper towel on the very edge of the enamel **[Q]**. This pulls the grains together and helps prevent air bubbles. Rinse the brush in the clean water and use it to remove any enamel grains that are out of place.

Place the pendant in a spot where it won't get bumped (some people use the top of the kiln). Let the enamel powder dry completely before firing. If moisture is left in the piece, it can boil and create bubbles in the enamel.

Fire the enamel

Firing will take approximately 3 minutes at 1472°F (800°C) but the time may vary from kiln to kiln. Firing times will also differ for different brands and colors of enamel. Experimentation and experience will help you get to know your enamels.

Position the piece as level as possible and fire until glossy. Cool and repeat the filling

process for the radiating shapes in yellow [R] and fire again. Cool. Repeat to add a thin layer of red enamel over the yellow in the center circle only. Cool. Polish the piece.

Mix up a small cup of liver of sulfur solution and fill two cups with clean, hot water.

> I add one teaspoon of ammonia to the hot LOS solution to help build up beautiful colors in the patina.

Dip the piece into the first cup of hot water to warm it, and then dip it into the LOS solution and then the other cup of hot water. Repeat this process to build up the color to a beautiful, dark blue. Rinse very well under running water and dry.

Use a jewelry polishing cloth to polish the back of the piece well. Wrap the polishing cloth over your fingertip and, using the back of your fingernail, lightly rub the top of the piece so only the silver wires and the high spots of the pattern are polished, leaving the patina in the recesses.

Michael Thee, Bronze Fern-Triangle, 2010. Sterling silver, bronze, rhodolite garnet, and patina of liver of sulfur, ammonia, and salt. Photo by the artist.

Ann Jenkins, Hot Totem Earrings, 2010. Fine silver, vitreous enamel, sterling silver. Photo by the artist.

Prairie blossom

This bracelet incorporates a bit of everything—three colorful polymer clay beads, a pod woven with seed beads, and two flower beads, flower disks, and a flower-shaped clasp made of fine-silver clay. A leaf-shaped toggle bar made of polymer clay is the finishing touch. All these components combine to create a fanciful medley of delicious colors and textures.

color

Medium/technique
Polymer clay, seed beads

Tools & supplies
- Polymer clay: ¹⁄₁₆ oz. each of 4 colors
- ¼ teaspoon pearlescent powder (metallic gold)
- Pasta machine or polymer clay roller
- Soft-bristled artist's paintbrush
- Craft oven and polyester batting
- Clear acrylic floor finish
- ¼ gram 15º seed beads in raspberry AB (color A) and tangerine orange transparent rainbow (color B)
- 2 grams 11º seed beads, transparent rainbow lime green (color C)
- 2 grams 8º seed beads in Siam Iris AB (color D) and frosted transparent rainbow moss green AB (color E)
- 22 11º seed beads, metallic bronze (color F)
- 10 8º seed beads, metallic bronze (color G)
- 16 6º seed beads, metallic bronze (color H)

Metal clay
• 25 grams fine-silver clay

Metal clay toolkit (p. 7)

Additional tools & supplies
• 2 19mm round bisque beads
• 3 16mm round wood beads
• Round wooden toothpick cut in half
• Cocktail straw cut to 1" (26mm)
• Circle cutters (⅜"/10mm and ⅝"/16mm)
• Flower-shaped clay cutters or
  templates (about ⅞"/22mm and
  1¼"/32mm)
• Cup of vermiculite
• Fireline 6-lb. test or similar thread
• #12 beading needle
• 4 2mm sterling silver crimp beads
• 12" (31cm) heavyweight beading wire
• 1½–2" 20-gauge sterling silver ball-end
  headpin
• 2" (51cm) 18-gauge sterling silver wire
• 4mm brass disk bead (for the back of
  the toggle)
• Crimping pliers
• Jewelry pliers (roundnose, flatnose,
  and chainnose)
• Flush cutters

Thoroughly condition the polymer clay
by running it through a pasta machine or
kneading and rolling it until it is soft and
pliable. Custom-blend the clay colors to
match or complement the colors of your
seed beads: I made clay sheets in bright
blue, dark red, orange, and lime green. Roll
each of the four clay colors to a thickness of
about 4 cards/1mm.

Cover the wood beads
Cut a strip of polymer clay wide enough to
cover the center portion of a 16mm wood
bead and long enough to wrap around the
bead. With the craft knife at a slight angle,
slice into the strip to bevel the end **[A]**. Trim
the excess clay from the end and wrap the
strip around the bead, overlapping the ends.

Grasp the bead at the top and bottom and
use your finger or a clay shaper to smooth
the seam where the ends overlap. Then
smooth and thin the clay near the bead's
top and bottom hole to about 1 card/.25mm.
Repeat to cover the two remaining wood
beads using different colors of clay **[B]**.

Create bead caps
Using contrasting colors of clay, cut out
flower shapes with a template or disk cutter.
Make a hole in the center of each flower
with a cocktail straw. Press a flower cap
onto each end of the covered beads. Roll

half a round toothpick vertically from the
hole down each petal to adhere the bead
caps to the base layer of clay. Make sure
you don't create air pockets between the
layers. With the pointed end of the toothpick,
impress lines between the petals **[C]**.

To embellish the bead caps, use the ⅝"
(16mm) circle cutter to cut six disks from
contrasting clay colors. Place a disk on
each bead cap and add texture with the cut
end of the toothpick, applying firm pressure
at the edges to adhere each disk tightly.
With the pointed end of the toothpick,
impress lines following those between the
petals. Finally, texture the body of the bead
using both the flat and pointed ends of the
toothpick. Clean up the bead holes on both
ends of each bead using the toothpick
[D]. Use the soft-bristled brush to apply
an extremely light dusting of pearlescent
powder to each bead **[E]**. Too much will
obscure the clay colors. Set aside.

Make the leaf toggle bar
Roll lime green polymer clay for the toggle
bar to 6 cards/1.5mm thick. With a craft
knife, cut a leaf shape about 1½" (38mm)
long. Use a needle tool to add details **[F]**.
Roll scraps of the remaining colors to
4 cards/1mm thick. Cut a small leaf from the
dark red and the orange clay. Use a small

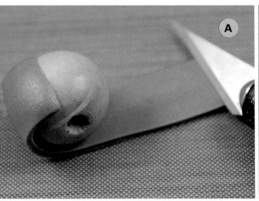

circle cutter (about ⅜"/10mm) to cut a disk from the bright blue clay.

Layer the small leaves on the large leaf and place the disk on top. Impress veins on the small leaves and create petal detailing on the disk. Use a needle tool to pierce a small hole through the center of the toggle bar. Smooth any rough or uneven edges. Finish with a light dusting of pearlescent powder **[G]**. Bake the toggle bar and the beads on polyester quilt batting in a craft oven following the polymer clay manufacturer's instructions. Remove from the oven and let the beads cool completely. Brush a thin coat of acrylic finish on each piece and let dry completely.

Make the metal clay beads

Roll the metal clay to 2 cards/.5mm thick. As you did with the polymer beads, cut the metal clay sheet and cover the two 19mm bisque beads, being sure to brush a bit of water between the overlapping ends of the metal clay to help them adhere. Let the beads dry completely **[H]**. Sand any imperfections with an ultra-fine sanding sponge. Set aside.

Make the metal clay toggle loop and disks

Roll the metal clay to 4 cards/1mm thick and texture as desired. Either working freehand or using a 1¼" (32mm) flower-shape cutter,

cut a flower shape for the toggle loop. With a ⅝" (16mm) circle cutter, cut a hole in the center of the flower. Use the smaller flower cutter to cut four flower disks or cut them freehand with your craft knife. Using a cocktail straw, make a hole in the center of each flower disk.

If you'd like the clasp and disks to have a curved surface, dry them textured side up on a light bulb or other form.

Cut two small round disks using the cocktail straw, stack them on top of one another, and flatten them with your finger until they are twice the size. Make a hole in the center with the pointed end of a toothpick **[I]**.

Let the metal clay pieces dry thoroughly. Smooth any rough edges with a fine-grit sanding sponge before firing. Place the metal clay beads and other pieces on a bed of vermiculite on a kiln shelf and fire following the manufacturer's directions. Let them cool completely. Polish by hand with a steel brush or use a polishing pad if you prefer a high shine. If you want an antique finish on your pieces, dip them in a liver of sulfur solution (warm water and a pea-sized piece of crushed liver of sulfur) until the desired color is achieved.

String the beads

This bracelet will fit an average-size wrist. Add or subtract 8° and 6° seed beads to adjust the length. Be sure to measure as you string the beads.

On 12" (31cm) of heavyweight beading wire, string a crimp bead, a 6° (color H) seed bead, an 8° (G), 11 11°s (F), and the clasp. Form a loop by going back through the 8°, the 6°, and the crimp bead, leaving a 1" (26mm) tail. Crimp the bead firmly with crimping pliers. String another crimp bead ½" (13mm) from the first. Crimp this bead firmly and cut off the excess wire. String a polymer clay bead, two 6°s, a flower disk, two 6°s, a flower disk, two 6°s, a flower disk, and two 6°s **[J]**.

String a polymer clay bead, a 6°, a metal clay bead, a 6°, a polymer clay bead, a 6°, and a metal clay bead. String two 6°s, a flower disk, two 6°s, two 8°s, a crimp bead, two 8°s, a crimp bead, two 8°s, a 6°, an 8°, and 11 11°s. Pass the beading wire back through the 8°, 6°s, both crimp beads, the flower disk, and the remaining 6°s. Leave just enough play in the wire so the bracelet will flex. Cut the wire, leaving a ½" (13mm) tail, and tuck the tail into the metal clay bead. Crimp both crimp beads **[K]**.

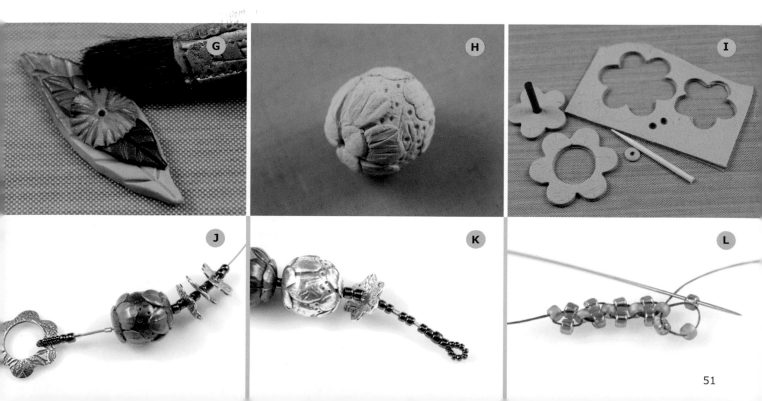

Stitch the right-angle weave pod bead

Row 1: Thread a #12 beading needle with a wingspan of conditioned Fireline. Working in right-angle weave, string four beads: an A, a B, an A, and a B. Go back through the first three beads strung, exiting an A, and pull the thread taut to form a unit. For the rest of the row, string three beads per unit instead of four. String a B, an A, and a B. Pass through the closest A from the initial set of beads, then pass through the B and A beads of the second set. String another B, A, and B set, pass through the A bead from the previous set of beads, and then pass through the B and A beads of the new set. Continue in the established pattern until you have five Bs at the bottom of the row, six As in the middle of the row, and five Bs at the top of the row. End this row with the needle exiting the last top B **[L]**.

> It's wise to always count your beads at the end of a row to make sure your pattern is correct. Doing this will save you time unweaving mistakes!

Row 2: String an A, a B, and an A. Pass through the last top B from the first row again. Pass through the A, B, and As that were just strung and pull the thread taut. Note that from here on you will always string three beads at the start of each row and two beads for the rest of the row. Pass through the next top B from row 1 and string an A and B. Pass down through the A from the previous unit and through the B and A of the second unit **[M]**. Pull the thread taut. Continue to the end of the row. Finish the row by passing through the top B.

Row 3: Turn the work. String three 11º Cs and pass through the B from the previous row and the three Cs again. Pass through the second top B from the previous row, string two Cs, and pass through the next C strung in the previous set, the top B from the previous row, and the following C side bead. Continue working across the row in the established pattern **[N]**.

Row 4: Work the fourth row with color-D 8ºs **[O]**.

Row 5: String an E, a D, and an E, and pass through the first top D from the previous row and through the E, D, and Es that were just strung. Pass through the second top D from the previous row, and string a D and an E. Pass through the next D, across through the top D from the previous row, and up through the E. Continue in the established pattern to the end of the row **[P]**.

Row 6: String a D, a C, and a D. Pass through the top D from the previous row and up through the beads that were just strung. Pass through the next top D and string a D and a C. Pass down through the D from the previous unit, through the top bead from the previous row, and up through the following D. Continue in the established pattern to the end of the row **[Q]**.

Row 7: Use Cs and Bs in row 7. A mirror-image pattern of the first four rows will emerge and the beads will start to pull in **[R]**.

Rows 8 & 9: Work rows 8 and 9 using Bs and As **[S]**. Repeat rows 3–9 for a total of three pattern repeats. Repeat rows 3–6 **[T]**.

Bring both ends of the strip together so they meet. Join the ends by working another row using 11ºs and passing through the

first row of the first segment as follows: string a C, pass through the bottom B of the first row, string a C, and pass through the top C from the last row. Pass through the C, B, and C beads again. Pass through the next top C from the last row, string a C, and pass through the second B from the first row, through the next C, and through the top C from the last row. Continue in the established pattern **[U]**. End by exiting an 11º C next to an 8º D.

* Pass through the 8º end beads at one side of the woven strip, pulling the thread taut to snug up the smaller beads. Pass through these beads twice more, tying several half-hitch knots along the way to secure. Exit an 8º E. Push the sections of 15ºs into the center of the bead so the 8ºs are dominant. String two 11º Cs, skip the next two 8º Ds, and pass through the next 8º E. Repeat three more times, exiting an 8º E **[V]**. Pass through these beads again, pulling the thread taut and tying several half-hitch knots along the way to secure the row.

Slip the bead onto the end of the bracelet. Pass through the next two 11º Cs and string one 15º B. Repeat three more times, pulling the thread taut to snug up the beads. Pass through these beads one more time, tying several half-hitch knots along the way to secure. Pass through one 15º B, string two 15º As **[W]**, and pass through the next B. Repeat three more times, pulling the thread taut. Pass through these beads once more, pulling the thread taut and tying several half-hitch knots along the way to secure this final row. Work the opposite end in the same manner. Weave in any loose thread ends, tying half-hitch knots along the way to secure the threads. Clip the thread ends close to the work. With the unfinished bead on the bracelet, repeat the sequence starting with * at the opposite end.

Attach the toggle
On the 20-gauge ball-end headpin, string the small metal clay disk, the toggle, and the small brass disk bead. With roundnose pliers, make a loop close to the toggle base, leaving just enough room (about ⅛"/3mm) to make a wire wrap later **[X]**.

If you're new to wirework, practice making loops with copper wire before working with sterling silver.

Grasp the wire loop with pliers in your nondominant hand and use chainnose pliers to wrap the end of the wire firmly around the stem of the loop. Trim any excess wire with flush cutters and smooth the wire end with a file if necessary.

Using roundnose pliers, grasp the 2" (51mm) piece of 18-gauge sterling silver wire and make a loop at one end, leaving a ½" (13mm) tail. Pass the loop through the toggle loop and firmly wrap the tail around the wire stem. Make a second loop at the opposite end of the wire and pass it through the beaded end loop of the bracelet. Wrap the remaining wire around the stem **[Y]**. Trim any excess wire with flush cutters. Smooth the wire end with a file if necessary.

The toggle should slide through the hole in the clasp and sit upright **[Z]**. Use pliers to adjust the angle by bending the looped end if necessary.

Fantasy flower

I love working with natural shapes and textures. This flower pendant uses lab-created cubic zirconias (CZs) to provide the sparkle and color. CZs are easy to incorporate in metal clay and they're kiln-ready. In flower nomenclature, the CZs are the *anthers* on top of wire *filaments*— together making up the flower's *stamen*. In my flower, two shades of ruby-color stones in two sizes give the piece an organic look and add visual depth.

 color

Medium/technique
Fireable CZs

Supplies
• 25–30 2–3mm CZs in 2 colors

Metal clay
• 16 grams fine-silver clay
• Syringe clay

Metal clay toolkit (p. 7)

Additional tools & supplies
• Flush wire cutters
• Chainnose pliers
• Beads to use as clay supports
• Toothpick
• Needle stylus
• 20" (51cm) 22-gauge fine-silver wire

template (actual size)

Prepare the filaments

Cut the wire into 20 10–15mm segments. With chainnose pliers, make a tiny loop at the end of each wire segment **[A]** and slightly curve the remaining wire.

> The word "blob" is my favorite term for the rounded syringe clay shape you'll make in the next step. Make your blobs 1mm larger than the CZ you're setting.

Place a blob of syringe clay on top of a loop at the end of a wire segment **[B]**. Use the flat side of the brush to slightly flatten the top of the blob. Use tweezers to set a CZ on top and gently push it into the blob so the girdle (widest part) of the CZ sinks below the line of the clay **[C]**. Repeat to add CZs to the remaining wire segments. Dry. Fire the filament components according to the clay manufacturer's instructions.

Make the metal clay petals

Use the template provided (or create your own petal shape) to create a paper pattern. Roll all the clay to 3 cards/.75mm thick. Place the pattern on the clay and use a scalpel or craft knife to cut out the shape **[D]**. Repeat to make a total of five petals. Pinch the tip of each petal and prop it using beads to give it an organic shape. Let the pieces dry. Use a flexible sanding pad to sand the edges until they are smooth.

Arrange and slightly overlap the petals in a flower shape. Apply a large blob of syringe clay in the center of the flower **[E]**. Use the brush to spread the clay, making sure all the petals are joined **[F]**. Let dry. Reinforce the back with another blob. Let dry. Embellish the join with leaf-like shapes (the sepals of the flower) to connect all five petals and reinforce the shape further **[G]**.

Make the bail

Roll a gram of clay to 3 cards/.75mm thick. Cut a ⅝ x 3/16" (16 x 5mm) piece and wrap the clay around a generously greased toothpick **[H]**. Trim any excess clay. Let dry. Sand the bail. Use syringe clay to connect the bail to the back of the pendant **[I]**. Wet the back of the pendant. Sign with a needle stylus if desired **[J]**. Let dry. Gently sand over the signature to remove any sharp pieces.

Embellish the flower component

Set one or two CZs on each petal and connect them to the center with an organic line of syringe clay **[K]**. Use chainnose pliers

to bend and slightly flatten the ends of the filaments **[L]**. Make a small blob at the edge of the large central blob **[M]**.

Using tweezers, set a filament by pushing it into the dab of clay **[N]**. First set the outer circle with the longer filaments, and then proceed to the center to set the shorter filaments. Dry the piece.

Fire according to the clay manufacturer's instructions. Polish. Use chainnose pliers to gently rearrange the filaments if needed.

Liz Hall, Solstices, 2012. Sterling silver, polymer, iridescent media. Photo by the artist.

Barbara Briggs, Tide Pool Cuff, 2010. Bronze, seed beads, pearls. Photo by the artist.

Pushing polymer

Use your favorite polymer colors to style a one-of-a-kind cabochon that fits perfectly in its metal clay bezel. When a thin sheet of polymer is gently pushed through a metal cutout, it produces a pillowed form of the cutout's shape—similar to the process of die-forming metal with a hydraulic press.

color

Technique/medium
Polymer

Tools & supplies
- Pea-sized balls of polymer in colors of your choice; ½ oz. translucent for each color; white; black
- Clay roller
- Pasta machine
- ¾" (19mm) circle cutter
- Imitation silver leaf (optional)
- Wet/dry sandpaper for use with polymer, 400 to 1200 grit
- Sculpey liquid polymer
- Cornstarch

Metal clay
- 25 grams silver or other metal clay
- 1.5mm skew carver

Metal clay toolkit (p. 7)

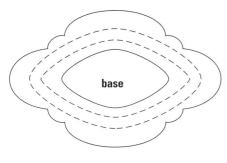

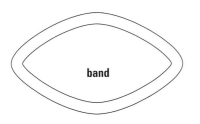

base

band

templates (actual size)

Prepare a design

Use the provided **templates** or draw a similar shape that has a cutout for the polymer clay cabochon. Allow room between the cutout and the outer edge for a slim band that will be added to the back. Transfer both templates onto an index card, cover the back of the index card with clear packing tape, and cut out the stencils with a craft knife.

Make the metal clay components

Roll 25 grams of metal clay to 4 cards/1mm thick, texture, and cut the base shape from the clay. Put the base on a warmer to dry.

Roll an untextured sheet of clay to 3 cards/.75mm thick and cut out the band stencil **[A]**. To make the bail, roll the remaining clay to 3 cards/.75mm thick and texture. Cut a strip ½" (13mm) wide and long enough to wrap around a straw or oiled brass tube. Wet and then secure the ends together **[B]**. (The seam doesn't need to have a neat finish because it will be removed later.) Set aside to dry. When the bail is semi-dry, carefully slide it off the tube and set on a warmer to fully dry. Sand and refine the three metal clay components.

Wet the area on the base where you will add the band. Wet one side of the band, firmly press the entire band onto the base, and hold for a minute to bond. Run a wet brush along the seam **[C]**.

Holding the bail on its side and cutting straight down, cut off one-third of the

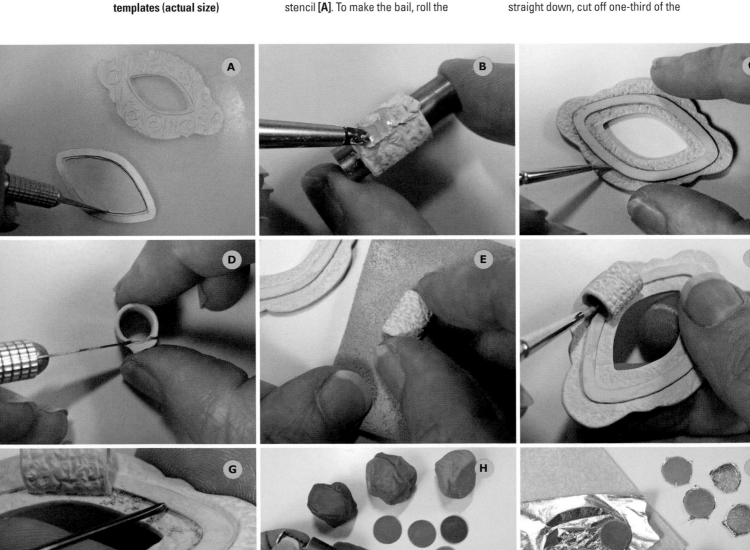

diameter, including the seam [D]. Sand the cut edges flat [E]. Attach the bail to the top center of the base. Reinforce with additional clay to smooth the join [F].

Undercut the band with a 1.5mm skew carver [G]. This will give the polymer clay an additional area to grip.

Fire following the metal clay manufacturer's instructions. Brush the piece with a brass brush and soapy water. Tumble and polish for a bright shine. Add patina if desired.

Make the polymer clay cabochon

Mix a pea-sized ball of each polymer clay color you'd like in your cabochon with ½ oz. translucent. Roll each mixed color into a sheet about 4 cards/1mm thick. Use a cutter to cut several disks from each color [H]. To add sparkle, back some or all of the polymer disks with imitation silver leaf [I]. Stack the disks in a random order. Compress the stack, and then cut it in half with a tissue blade [J]. Cut a slice from one of the halves and run it through the third-thickest setting of a pasta machine.

Using the pendant as a frame, determine what area of the polymer clay sheet you'd like to push through the cutout [K]. Trim away the excess clay on the back. Dip your finger into cornstarch to keep it from sticking, and then gently push the polymer clay through the frame into a cabochon shape. Look at the dome from different angles to make sure it's even [L]. On the back, tamp down the outer edges of the polymer clay with a ball stylus so it doesn't rise above the silver band [M].

Bake the cabochon in the frame with the top facing up according to the polymer clay manufacturer's instructions.

If you want the polymer to have a glossy shine, press the cabochon to pop it out of the silver frame. Wet-sand the polymer, starting with 400-grit and progressing to finer grits [N]. Buff for a final shine.

Put the cabochon back in the frame. Smear a tiny bit of liquid polymer over the back of the baked polymer. Cover it with a thin layer of white polymer clay. The white backing will keep the translucent colors bright [O].

Fill the rest of the back with black polymer clay. Shave off the excess with a tissue blade until the height is even with the metal band [P].

For a finishing touch, use a piece of coarse sandpaper to texture the back of the cabochon [Q]. Bake the entire piece for 30 minutes at the polymer clay manufacturer's recommended temperature.

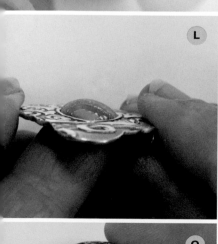

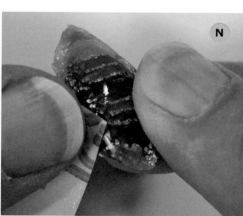

Beaded leaf

I once saw a photo of a jewelry piece that featured seed beads set in enamel, which made perfect sense to me: Enamel and seed beads are both glass, after all. I started experimenting to figure out the process. I developed this technique that uses lily root powder, an organic product that burns off in the kiln, to hold the beads in place until the enamel melts to permanently hold the beads. This pin easily adapts into a pendant.

color

Technique/medium
Tile-set seed beads

Tools & supplies
- 11º Czech seed beads in three shades of transparent green
- Bright pale green enamel (Ninomiya N41)
- Lily root powder or Klyr-Fire
- Dust mask
- Eyedropper
- Distilled water
- Fine-tip brush
- Kiln-safe wire rack or trivet
- Kiln tongs
- Beading needle

Metal clay
- 30 grams fine-silver clay
- Syringe clay

Metal clay toolkit (p. 7)

Additional tools & supplies
- Card stock
- Micro carving tool
- Isopropyl alcohol
- Fine-silver pin-back finding

template (actual size)

Make the templates

Use the **template** provided or create your own. Transfer two copies of the design onto card stock. Set one template aside as the base. For the other template, cut out the areas you want to fill with enamel and beads; this is the top template.

Make the metal clay base

Roll about 20 grams of clay to 3 cards/.75mm thick and large enough to accommodate the template. Place the base template on the clay, trace the template with a craft knife, and remove the excess clay. Allow the clay base to dry **[A]**.

Roll the remaining clay to 5 cards/1.25mm thick. Impress the top template into the clay and cut out the interior shapes. Cut around the outside of the template **[B]**. Let dry. Moisten and add syringe clay or paste to the top piece **[C]** . Position the top piece over the base and allow to dry **[D]**. Sand and refine the piece **[E]**. Use a carving tool to add crisp details **[F]**.

Attach the pin back finding

Determine the best place for the pin-back finding on the back of the piece. Mark the spots for the finding pieces with a pencil and carve recesses for them **[G]**. Rehydrate the clay, add syringe clay to the holes **[H]**, and press the findings in place. Smooth some clay over the base pieces and set aside to dry **[I]**. Texture the back with a rough paintbrush and slightly thick paste **[J]**.

Fire according to the metal clay manufacturer's instructions. Tumble-polish the fired piece and clean it thoroughly with isopropyl alcohol.

Clean the enamel

Put a small amount of enamel in a spoon and use an eyedropper to add several drops of distilled water [K]. Swish the water back and forth to stir up the finest grains ("fines"). Dump the cloudy water into an empty cup [L].

Wet-pack the enamels onto the base

Using a very fine-tipped brush, pick up a small amount of wet enamel and pack it into the recessed areas of the pendant [M]. Continue until the base is completely covered and thick enough for the seed beads to sink into when fired.

Level the enamel by tapping a brush handle against the side of the piece [N]. If the metal clay has sucked all the water out of the enamel, it will be hard to level. If this has happened, add a drop or two of water to the enamel and tap. If you have too much moisture, use a paper towel to wick the water out of the enamel. Allow the enamel to dry thoroughly.

Bring the kiln to between 1450–1500°F (788–816°C). Place the dried piece on a wire rack or trivet and use kiln tongs to transfer the rack into the kiln [O]. Close the door and fire for 2–3 minutes. Remove the piece from the kiln and cool.

Add lily root powder and seed beads

Prepare the lily root powder by adding a small amount of water to a little bit of powder. A little goes a long way. At first the powder will ball up; continue to stir while adding tiny drops of water [P]. Brush the powder lightly and evenly onto the enamel base, a small area at a time [Q], as it dries quickly. If it dries prior to adding the seed beads, simply remoisten with water; do not add more powder. Place seed beads into the moistened powder in the desired pattern. I use a beading needle to pick up and place a number of beads at a time [R]. Place the pendant face up on the wire rack [S].

Fire at enameling temperature for 2–3 minutes. Open the kiln door and crash cool to 1000°F (538°C). However, do not remove the piece from the kiln. Allow the kiln to come to room temperature, remove the piece, and repolish.

Add the pin stem

Cut the pin stem to fit the catch and sharpen the end with a file. Position the stem in the catch and tighten with pliers [T].

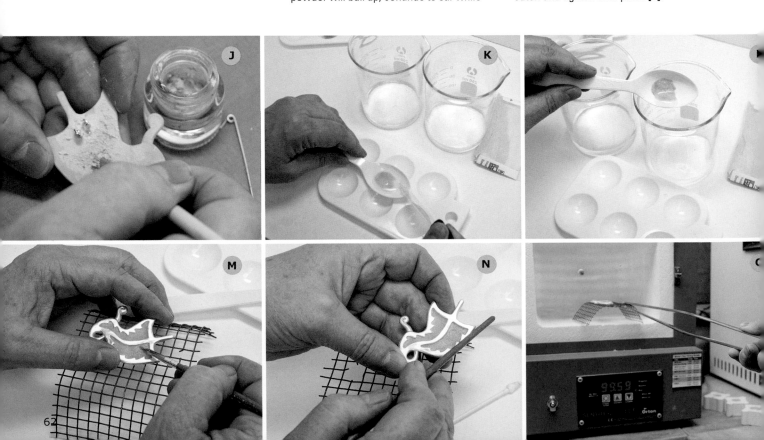

Tips for using seed beads

Although Klyr-Fire can be used to hold the seed beads on the enamel base, I find that lily root powder has the best hold. I have literally dropped pieces after the powder was dry and not had a seed bead move out of place. If applied too heavily, however, the lily root powder can leave a dirty look on light colors such as white or yellow.

Make sure you create a deep enough recess to hold a good layer of enamel as a base for the seed beads to sink into during firing. There are a couple of ways to set the seed beads. The first is to sink the seed beads in the bottom layer of enamel with one firing and leave it that way. The second is to lightly sift more enamel over the seed beads after the first firing for a smoother surface. I prefer to not use a second enamel coat; I feel it detracts from the look of the seed beads.

The type of seed bead you use is important. Test the beads prior to using them. Some colors will change in the kiln; for example, some pinks will turn brown. Also, effects such as iridescent coatings and silver linings will burn off. I like using Czech-made beads because they are more "bead" and less hole, whereas the Japanese beads have a larger hole and less glass. Japanese beads tend to collapse during firing, resulting in a flatter surface, which can be nice. Smaller beads allow for more bead placement and pattern, but take longer to set in place.

Another quirk of using so many seed beads in the enamel is that they behave like fused glass; you cannot remove the piece from the kiln until it comes to room temperature, otherwise the glass cools too fast and the seed beads will pop off the piece. My first attempt at using seed beads was a beautiful, detailed leaf. I removed it from the kiln and then wondered what the crackling sounds were. All the seed beads that I had spent hours putting in place had popped off the enamel. If you use only a few seed beads in an enameled piece, you can treat it just as any other enameled metal clay piece with no worries of beads popping off.

I like to plan geometric patterns on graph paper. The piece at the top uses tiny 15° seed beads.

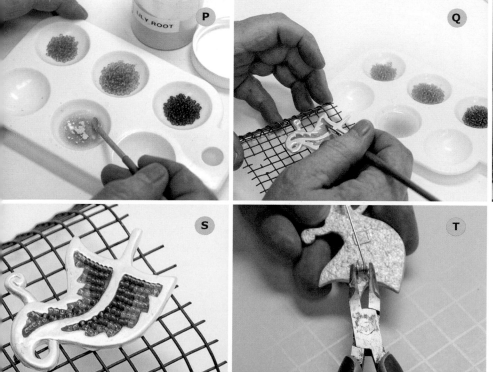

Textured feathers

Using sand as a creative medium is an ancient tradition that is still widely used today. Tibetan monks create intricate sand-filled mandalas, ritualistically destroying them after the ceremony as a symbol of the transitory nature of life. The Navajo people use beautiful sand paintings in healing rituals, and Australian Aborigines mix sand with mud and paint it onto bark. With the technique presented here, you'll build layers of color that are durable enough for jewelry.

color

Medium/technique
Colored sand inlay

Tools & supplies
- White sand
- Artists acrylic paints or water-based wall paint
- Baking dish
- Warming plate
- Disposable cups
- Wooden craft sticks
- Ceramic or glass containers
- Sieve
- Clear plastic storage containers with lids
- Fine-tip artificial bristle paintbrushes (00 and 000)
- Weldbond glue
- Toothpicks
- Medium-hard toothbrush

SUPPLIES
Metal clay
- 16 grams fine-silver clay

Metal clay toolkit (p. 7)

Additional tools & supplies
- Photopolymer plate or texture sheet that makes a 1mm deep impression
- Baby wipes
- 1" (26mm) 20-gauge (0.8mm) fine-silver wire
- Pair of earring wires

Choosing sand and pigments

Although you can use an array of purchased colors of sand for this project, you can easily, quickly, and cheaply color your own sand starting with white sand from a craft store, hardware store, or pet shop. I use natural white sand, but if that's not available, you may be able to find chemically whitened sand—the whiter the better.

Totally dry sand works best. To dry the sand, pour it into a large baking dish to a depth of no more than ½" (13mm) and set the dish on a warming plate on low to medium heat. The sand may get quite hot. Stir a few times until it flows easily.

Artists acrylic paints are easy to find and produce a full range of colors straight out of the tube. For a more personal color palette, mix the exact colors you want. Mix colors lighter and brighter than you want your final color to be; acrylics tend to dry darker and duller, and the sand can dull them even more. Water-based wall paints work fine too; sometimes they are available in sample pots or tubes. These are economical if you're planning to make large batches of colored sand.

Mix the colored sand

For my earrings, I mixed sand in bright fuchsia as a base, two lighter tints of fuchsia, and black for contrast. You can mix additional tints and contrasting colors if desired.

For the base color, put half a cup of dry white sand in a disposable cup and add a teaspoon of acrylic artists paint. (If you add too much paint, just add a little dry sand until the mix is right; you'll quickly develop a feel for the right consistency.)

Use a craft stick to thoroughly stir the paint into the sand **[A]**. Scrape the bottom of the cup frequently to mix in any dry sand that might be there.

Put a quarter cup of the base-color sand in a disposable cup, add a quarter cup of dry white sand, and stir well. This is your second color batch.

For a third tint, add a quarter cup of white sand to a quarter cup of sand from the second batch and stir. This last batch will be much dryer to mix than the previous two batches; adding a few drops of water will make it much easier to get the sand to take the color.

Transfer all the colors of sand into ceramic or glass containers. Put them on the warming tray to dry along with the stir sticks

[B]. Stir each pot every 20–30 minutes to keep the sand from clumping. As the sand dries, you'll see the grains separate and become free-flowing again.

Put the dry, colored sand through a sieve to eliminate any debris and to catch any small lumps that may have formed; pinch them between your fingers to break them up. You can crush hard lumps with a pestle and mortar.

Put the sand in storage containers. Clear containers make it easy see the colors as you work **[C]**.

I like to use a PPP (photopolymer plate) to make my metal clay pieces (see instructions on p. 68). With a PPP, I can get all my design elements exactly where I want them. You can use my templates to make plates for the front and back of the earrings [D] or design your own.

The earrings are made of two layers of textured metal clay. On the front, you'll build up a high, wide frame to hold the sand inlay. The walls of the frame need to be at least 1mm high to contain the sand and fairly thick so they are not obscured by grains of sand.

Create the top layers

Thoroughly oil the plate. Roll the clay to 6 cards/1.5mm thick. Reduce the thickness guides to 4 cards/1mm and place the oiled side of the plate on the clay. Roll over the plate to impress the design for the top layer in the clay. Remove the plate. Trim the excess clay. Repeat to make a second top layer. Let the pieces dry completely.

back (base layer)

front (top layer)

templates (actual size)

Using a texture plate for the backs creates lively contrast with the colorful, dramatic fronts.

Smooth the edges. Using a needle tool, scratch texture into the depressed areas that will hold the sand. The texture will provide tooth for better adhesion.

Use syringe clay or slender cylinders of rolled clay to build up the outer frame and dividing line. To add feather detail to the top, roll more clay, press it into the top (triangular) section of the plate, and trim **[E]**. Moisten the top layer, apply plenty of paste, and then gently press the feather detail in place. Use sculpting tools to model some extra definition to the feather detail while the clay is wet **[F]**. Use a soft, wet brush to smooth any tool marks and to neaten the join between the layers. Repeat to make a second layered piece. Let the pieces dry without heat for 15–20 minutes.

Make the earring loops and base layers

Mark the center top of the back. Shape ½" (13mm) of fine-silver wire into a half loop and bend the ends of the wire slightly so the loop will be held securely. Using the same thickness guides as before, roll the remaining clay on the plate and trim the outline to create a base layer. (The textured side is the back of the earring.) Apply a little water to the back of the dry top layer, add some paste, and join the two pieces, trapping the wire **[G]**. Press gently to join. Neaten the edges and allow to dry completely. Repeat to make a second earring.

Check the finished pieces for imperfections. Wipe the pieces gently and briefly with a baby wipe; this removes fine scratches and dust and leaves a very smooth finish **[H]**. Let dry thoroughly.

Fire following the metal clay manufacturer's instructions. Apply a patina, and polish to your favorite finish. If you are using dark colors of sand, leave the patina very dark in the depressions where the sand will go **[I]**.

Apply the colored sand

Set up your workspace with colored sand, glue, brushes, and some rinse water for the brushes. I work over a piece of white copy paper to make it easy to return any spilled sand back into its container. Use a very fine permanent marker to draw lines on the metal to guide the placement of the colored sand. You'll apply a base layer of sand, let dry overnight, and then apply a top layer of sand.

Use a very fine-tipped brush to apply glue to the first color area. Depending on the intricacy of the design, you may have to use a brush as fine as #000. Use your fingers to pick up and sprinkle the first color of sand onto the glued area all at once. Don't give the glue a chance to pull back from the edges of the design.

Very lightly press the sand into the glue and tap off the excess. Inspect the outline of the sand area. If any sand needs to be pushed back in line, use a toothpick to do so before the glue gets too dry.

Apply more glue to any areas that need the same color of sand and apply the sand. Let each glued color dry for about 30 minutes before applying another color **[J]**. (While the glue is wet, it could pick up specks of another color; they are very tedious to remove!) Let dry overnight.

Apply the second layer of color
The second layer of color will be applied with thinned glue: Dispense some glue into a clean cup and add a few drops of water, aiming for a light, creamy consistency. You want the glue to flow into the sand layer,

but it should not be so thin that it loses its bonding power. Again use a very fine brush to apply the glue and avoid the outside edges of each color so the sand domes slightly between the colors. (If you prefer a flat look, go all the way to the edge of the underlying color.)

Apply the thinned glue and sprinkle the sand in the same manner as before **[K]**. Apply one color at a time and let it dry for 30 minutes before applying another color.

After all the colors are applied, let the piece dry overnight. Brush the piece with a medium-hard toothbrush to remove any loose grains of sand. Add earring wires to complete the earrings.

An optional step that gives the piece a slightly glossy look is to apply a thin layer of watered-down glue over the sand to seal the design; this will prevent particles of sand from coming loose.

Holly Gage, Jewelry That Rocks!, 2011. *Fine silver, CD, sterling silver. Photo by the artist.*

Patrik Kusek, untitled, 2012. *Fine silver, resin, copper foil, gold foil, paint swatch. Photo by Pancho San Benito.*

Pam East, Eternal Flame, 2011. *Fine silver, gold foil, enamel, sterling silver. Photo by the artist.*

Texture plates

Tools & supplies
- Metal shears (steel plates) or scissors (plastic plates)
- Photopolymer plate (PPP), steel or plastic
- Artwork printed on a transparency or tracing paper
- UV exposure unit
- Digital timer
- Nail brush or other firm brush
- Soft sponge or paper towel
- Hair dryer
- Vegetable oil

Exposure frame
- Masonite board (2 x 2"/51 x 51mm larger than the artwork)
- Bubble wrap or thin foam
- Tape
- 2mm thick glass the same size as the Masonite board
- Clamps

UV lamps designed as nail polish dryers (top photo) work for making PPPs. A large unit will be the most versatile. You can make a portable exposure unit like mine from a toolbox fitted with UV tubes (bottom photo). Everything is inside—easy to store away and ready to go in a flash.

As you reach a certain point in your development as an artist, you may want the textures you incorporate to reflect your own aesthetic and come from your own hand. This will likely mean putting aside purchased stamps and texture sheets in favor of creating your own. By making photopolymer plates from artwork you've created, you can begin developing a signature style for your jewelry line.

Photopolymer plates, also called PPPs or solar plates, are made of a light-sensitive polymer layer on a metal or plastic backing. To make a photopolymer texture plate, you expose the photopolymer plate and your design printed on a transparency sheet to UV light. The black areas of your design block the light and keep the polymer soft. UV light passes through the clear areas of the design, hardening the polymer beneath those areas. You wash away the soft

sections (this creates the recessed areas of the plates), leaving the hardened areas on the plate raised.

What kind of plates should I use?
The detail in your artwork and the depth of the impression required will help you determine what type of plate to use. My preference overall is for steel-backed plates: The polymer layer is harder, and they hold fine lines beautifully. When a shallow texture is your goal (such as for keum-boo), use the thinnest plate available (I use a 0.9mm plate). For medium-depth work, I recommend plates that are 1.45mm thick. These are great all-purpose plates. For enamel work, where a deep texture is best, use plates that are 1.75mm thick. These thick plates are a little harder to find (see

Sources and resources, p. 111). Plastic-backed plates are softer and do not hold very fine detail, but they are easier to cut than the steel-backed plates. They are great for bold designs.

Prepare a design
All artwork for PPPs must be high-contrast black and white. No gray areas are allowed!

Think in reverse to anticipate how your art will translate to the finished metal piece. Black areas or lines in the artwork will become the raised areas of the metal clay piece. White (clear areas on the transparency) areas will be the recessed areas of the metal clay piece (dark if you apply patina). Text must be flipped so it reads in reverse on the plate. Avoid fine lines, especially if you are using a thicker plate. It can be very hard to get clay out of thin grooves.

Print your design on a standard overhead transparency. Make sure the transparency film is compatible with the printer used. For best results, make two transparency copies and layer them, keeping the design perfectly in register.

You can also use two layers of regular tracing paper. Another option is to use thermal negative film, which can be exposed and developed using the same UV exposure unit as for the plates. This film produces a dense black and gives very sharp results. It's especially useful when making fine detail plates, or artwork with text.

Make a test strip and prepare the frames
Copy my test strip or create your own strip of numbers from 1 to 5. Make two prints on transparency film, trim them, and sandwich the pieces together with clear sticky tape.

```
1 1 1 1 1   2 2 2 2 2   3 3 3 3 3   4 4 4 4 4   5 5 5 5 5
1 1 1 1 1   2 2 2 2 2   3 3 3 3 3   4 4 4 4 4   5 5 5 5 5
1 1 1 1 1   2 2 2 2 2   3 3 3 3 3   4 4 4 4 4   5 5 5 5 5
1 1 1 1 1   2 2 2 2 2   3 3 3 3 3   4 4 4 4 4   5 5 5 5 5
```

Test strip

Tape a piece of bubble wrap to the board (bubbles down/smooth side up). Gather the 2mm glass and clamps.

An inexpensive photo frame that has a sturdy backing can be disassembled and used to make your exposure frame.

How to determine the right exposure time

Keep the plates away from sunlight or any UV light source. The plates can be handled safely in any non-UV light. Keep the plates upside down. Fluorescent room lights are fine for short periods.

Please note the exposure times given are a guide only. You may have to expose a test strip a few times to determine the best exposure for your light setup and plate type.

Cut a 1 x 5½" (25mm x 14cm) strip off the plate. Remove and discard the cover film. Position the test-strip artwork on the plate. Place the plate in the center of the exposure frame, cover it with the glass sheet, and clamp the assembly together (avoiding the design). Use a piece of cardboard to cover all of the plate except the last 1" (25mm). Expose this area for 15 seconds.

Turn off the light, reset the timer for another 15 seconds, move the card another inch, and expose again. Repeat the process until the whole test strip has been exposed. The final exposure will receive only 15 seconds of light, the next 30, the next 45 seconds, and so on.

Clean the plate

Wash the plate in a shallow tray of warm water, scrubbing with a nail brush in a circular motion until you can feel clean metal. Any photopolymer left on the metal will feel a bit slippery.

You can now judge the perfect exposure time for your light source. Look for the

section of numbers that has very smooth, crisp edges and a complete washout, right to the base metal. An overexposed area will be very hard to wash out; thin lines may not wash out at all, and nothing will wash out cleanly to the base metal. Underexposed areas will wash away too much, leaving soft, rounded edges and wider lines than the original design, and sometimes entire areas may disappear.

As a reference point, a medium-thick plate takes 85 seconds and a very thin plate takes 75 seconds for the perfect exposure using my UV exposure unit (with new UV tubes).

Make the plate

Prepare the transparencies of the design. If you are using steel-backed plates, use good-quality metal shears to cut the plate to the size of the design. Plastic plates can be cut with heavy-duty household scissors. Remove and discard the film that covers the plate. Layer the transparencies, the plate, and the exposure frame, and clamp the

glass over the top **[A]**. Turn on the lamp and expose the plate for the optimum time.

Remove the plate and scrub it in the tray of warm water **[B]**. If your design has thin lines, leave a little bit of material on the base metal to hold the line; thin lines have a tendency to lift off the metal base. This polymer will be hardened in a second exposure. Wipe off the excess water with a soft sponge. Dry the plate with a hair dryer. The plate is dry when it doesn't feel sticky anymore. Take care not to overheat the plate; the polymer layer can separate from its backing.

Expose the plate again for the same length of time as the initial exposure. This will harden the plate all the way through, including any soft particles that were exposed during the washout process. Brush a little vegetable oil over the whole plate to prevent drying and cracking.

Ideas for PPPs

- **Design a texture from your own drawings or doodles.** Use them as they are or scale them up or down to make related pieces using the same design.
- **Use text, handwriting, or calligraphy.** Be sure to mirror the image so that it reads correctly on your finished piece.
- **Create a logo or makers mark.**
- **Convert a photo to a high-contrast black-and-white image.**

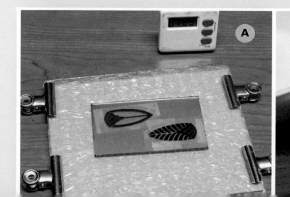

Brilliant fibula

Originally worn to fasten clothing, the fibula is an ancient form of brooch that usually includes a hinge or spring. This pin has plenty of surface area where you explore a combination of water etching and enameling. In water etching, you paint a wax resist directly onto the surface, so an organic, one-of-a-kind design is almost guaranteed. Enameling the recesses of the etched design adds a brilliant and colorful accent to the fibula.

color

Medium/technique
Water etching and enameling

Tools & supplies
- 80-mesh medium-temperature, medium expansion transparent enamel for silver*
- 4 x 6" coated card stock
- Klyr-Fire (optional for flat surfaces, recommended for rounded or domed surfaces)
- Small glass jar
- Distilled water
- Container lined with paper towel or coffee filter
- Enamel spatula
- Enamel spreader
- Paintbrush for enamel (must be new/clean and dedicated to enamel)
- Diamond sanding sticks or paper
- Optional—fine-grit alundum stone
- Glass brush
- Safety glasses
- Dust mask
- Gloves

Blue, green, and purple enamels work best on silver.

Metal clay

- 25 grams fine-silver clay (I get the best etching results with PMC+)
- Fine-silver clay paste

Metal clay toolkit (p. 7)

Additional tools & supplies

- 1mm and 2mm drill bits
- Cotton swabs or paper towel
- 6" (15cm) 16-gauge half-hard sterling silver wire
- Pencil
- Water-soluble wax resist
- Paintbrush for wax
- Soft silk sea sponge
- File or fish hook sharpener
- 3M Tri-M-Ite sandpapers in various grits
- Trivet
- Wire rack
- Firing fork
- Heatproof surface
- Jewelry pliers (chainnose, roundnose)
- Flush cutters

Enameling techniques

This project showcases filled recesses with a low relief design beneath the enamel. It combines the techniques of **champlevé**, in which depressions in the metal are filled with enamel and fired, with **basse-taille** enameling, in which the metal surface has a textured pattern or design over which the enamel is fired.

Make the body of the pin

Roll clay for the back plate to 3 cards/.75mm thick. Cut out the base shape using a triangle template if desired or freehand **[A]**. Cut smaller accent triangle shapes from the excess clay sheet. Dry the pieces on a mug warmer or in a dehydrator, turning often to minimize warping.

Roll clay for the etched top plate to 5 cards/ 1.25mm thick and cut to fit within the base shape **[B]**. Dry in the same way as the base.

Roll a cylinder of clay the thickness of a lollipop stick, which is ⁵⁄₃₂" (4mm) **[C]**. Cut the cylinder into two ³⁄₁₆" (5mm) pieces and allow these to dry completely. With a 1mm drill bit, drill a pilot hole through the end of each cylinder to create a tube. Enlarge the holes using a 2mm drill bit **[D]**.

Cut or file off the side of each tube just at the outside edge of the hole to form a flat side for attaching to the back (this will resemble a letter C). Cut just up to the edge of the hole to keep the 2mm opening the proper size for the pin finding.

Sand any rough edges **[E]**. To assemble, moisten the areas where the clay will be attached with water. Use paste to join the pieces, making sure that all joins are well sealed and tidy **[F]**.

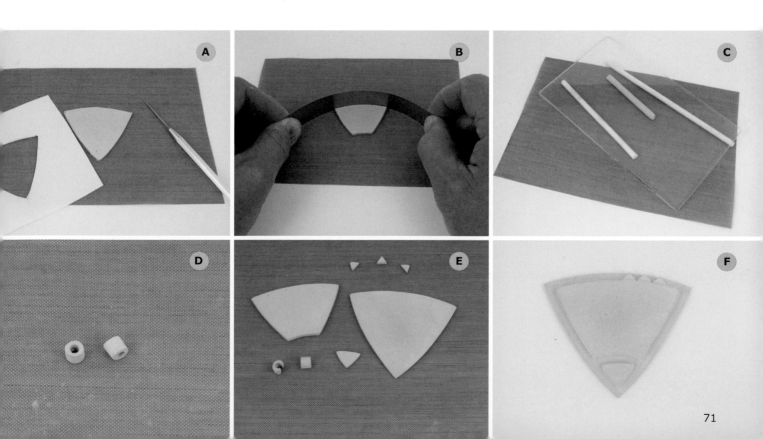

On the back of the base, attach the two C-shaped loops as shown [G]. Placement of the loops affects the center of gravity, so do not place them too low. Dry the whole piece.

Using a pencil, draw the design for etching on the dry clay. For a two-layer etch, draw only the outside border and the areas you want to be high silver lines. These are the areas that you'll paint resist onto; areas that are not painted with wax will wash away.

Apply the wax resist
Pour a small amount of wax onto a piece of coated card stock (old postcards work well). Close the bottle of wax; it dries out when exposed to air.

Paint the pencilled design with the wax using a fairly loaded brush [H]. If the wax is too thin, it may come off in the etching process. Keep a cup of hot water nearby for rinsing the wax brush. Dry the brush on a paper towel before returning to the wax; you don't want to dilute the wax.

Paint wax onto all parts that will not be etched, including the exposed areas of the base and the back [I]. This prevents fingerprints while handling and keeps the joins from loosening while the piece is wet.

Be careful not to press too hard and risk cracking or breaking the loops on the back of the pendant.

Allow the wax to air-dry thoroughly for at least 2 hours; do not use a mug warmer or a dehydrator, which can melt the wax. Use a craft knife to remove unwanted wax and to clean up the lines before etching [J].

Using a paintbrush moistened with water, gently brush the surface of the clay [K]. Use a wet silk sponge to wipe away the loosened clay [L]. For even etching, avoid concentrating the brush in any one area. Wring the sponge into water to recover the etched clay. Wipe the sponge in all directions to keep the edges of the lines as vertical as possible. Wiping only in one direction creates a slope on one side for the recess and may undercut the other.

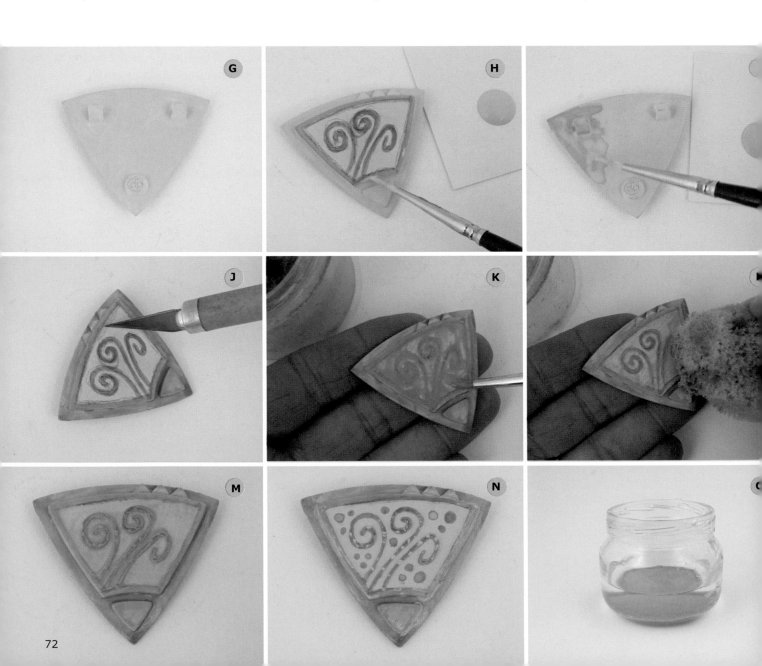

Repeat the process until the desired amount of clay has been removed (about 1 card/.25mm, not including the thickness of the wax). Air-dry the piece again **[M]**. If the depth is difficult to judge, allow the piece to dry thoroughly and check; continue etching if more depth is needed. Dry the piece again.

For a second etched layer, paint wax onto the dry clay for the areas where you want a basse-taille effect **[N]**. Allow the wax to dry and repeat the etching process. Remove about another half card; this etch does not need to be as deep as the first. Allow the piece to dry thoroughly before firing.

Be sure your kiln is in a well-ventilated area. Support the piece on a fiber blanket and fire for an hour or more according to the clay manufacturer's instructions. If the piece warps during firing, gently reshape it. Tumble-polish the piece for 2 hours or until the surface is shiny. Do not over tumble or you may soften the lines. Rinse with distilled water. Avoid handling the etched surface of the piece to prevent contamination with skin oils.

Prepare the enamel

Spoon about 1 tsp. of enamel into the jar. Fill the jar about halfway with tap water. Gently swirl the jar, allow the water to settle for about 10 seconds, and pour the cloudy water into a container lined with a paper towel or coffee filter to prevent enamel from going down the drain. Repeat the washing process three or four times until the water is clear **[O]**, and then use distilled water to wash one or two more times. Leave a few drops of the distilled water in the enamel. Wrap the paper towel/filter and place in the trash (or save it to use as counter-enamel in another project). This is a good time to preheat your kiln (see box at left).

Apply the enamel

Using the spatula and spreader, place wet enamel into the recesses **[P]**. (Some people prefer using a paintbrush for this step.) Including a little water with each scoop of enamel makes application easier; too

Enameling tips from Catherine

The method used for filling the etched area with enamel is called wet-packing. Working with wet enamel minimizes airborne enamel dust. Enamels contain metal oxides and other components that should not be inhaled. Exercise caution and wear a safety mask when handling dry enamel powder.

Enamel provides a beautiful palette of color for use on metal clay. Because some colors (especially reds and oranges) turn yellow in contact with silver, areas in direct contact with the silver like the etched recesses should not be filled with these colors. When in doubt, test the color first. A few other tips:
- Use clean tools dedicated to enameling.
- Make sure your work area is clean and free of oils or metal clay contamination.
- Preheat the kiln to 1450°F (788°C).
- For clear, brilliant transparent enamel, it's important to wash the enamel thoroughly to remove the "fines"—the fine particles created in the grinding process. It's best to wash only what you will need immediately; washed enamel can degrade over time.

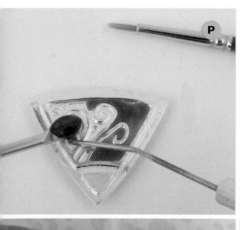

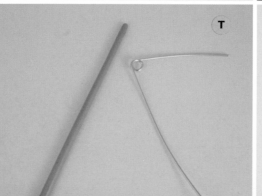

much water makes it difficult to control the placement of the enamel. Fill the recesses evenly and don't overfill [Q]. For best results, enamel should be applied in layers. Too much enamel in any one layer may cause bubbles or pits to form.

Hold the piece by the edges and gently tap the sides with the handle of one of the tools to level the enamel. Use a cotton swab (or paper towel) to press lightly against one edge of the enamel to wick away excess water. Allow the enamel to dry before firing (you'll know it's dry when it returns to the powdered color).

Remove any stray grains of enamel on any surface other than the etched face (which will be sanded or "stoned" down). After firing, the grains will be difficult to remove.

Place your piece on the trivet (or directly on a clean, enamel-free wire mesh rack). Carefully use the firing fork to lift and place the entire assembly into the kiln. Work quickly to minimize heat loss.

Opening the kiln door causes the temperature to drop significantly. When the temperature returns to 1450°F (788°C), time for 2 minutes. Check the piece to see if the enamel has become smooth. If not, leave it for another 10–15 seconds and check again. The timing of enameling is not exact; many factors come into play, including the size and thickness of the silver, the weight of the mesh, and the length of time the door is open.

When the enamel is smooth, remove the entire assembly from the kiln and place it onto a heatproof surface to cool. Do not remove the piece from the mesh or trivet too soon to avoid thermal shock.

Apply more enamel

Repeat the wet-packing and firing steps until the enamel is just above the surface of the silver. This may take three or four firings.

When the piece is cool, use diamond-grit sanding sticks under running water to grind the enamel level with the silver surface [R]. Move from coarse to fine. Rinse and clean the surface with a glass brush between grits and after you reach the finest grit [S]. Rinse the piece with distilled water and allow it to dry. When dry, the surface will appear matte with very fine scratches. Apply a small amount of enamel to fill any shiny spots, which are low spots, before firing.

Return the piece to the kiln for a final firing to smooth the enamel surface. After firing, you can use 3M Tri-M-Ite wet/dry sanding papers (600-grit or finer) to finish the surface of the silver without damaging the enamel. Tumble-polish the piece if desired.

Make the pin finding

Determine the length of the pin stem and allow room for sharpening the point (a little extra length is insurance at this point; it can be trimmed before sharpening). Bend the sterling silver wire around a small mandrel or paintbrush handle, or use roundnose pliers to create the spring [T].

Pass the wire end without the spring through both loops on the back of the pendant. Using chainnose and roundnose pliers, bend the wire as shown [U] to properly position the spring and form the clasp. Trim the excess wire and sand the catch end until smooth. Pull up on the pin if more spring is needed to fit into the catch.

File the stem to a point and finish it with sandpaper to a smooth, evenly tapered end [V]. This style of pin is not suitable for wearing on delicate fabrics because of the thick pin stem.

(V)

Vickie Hallmark, Moonbird, 2009. Fine silver, Faux Bone, resin, rainbow topaz. Photo by the artist.

Lorena Angulo, Tree of Life, 2009. Bronze, gesso, acrylic paint. Photo by George Post.

Patrik Kusek, untitled, 2010. Fine silver, cement, resin, soft coral, carnelian, agate. Photo by Drew Davidson.

Medusa's garden

These earrings get color in several ways: a sparkling central gemstone, deep patina from liver of sulfur, and an unusual source—tinted cement. Because the cement starts out rather gray, it was tricky to find a pigment that gave it enough color and didn't change its consistency to make it too dry or too wet. After a lot of experimentation, I landed on an easy-to-find, hardware-store brand of cement and a common artists paint that worked beautifully.

color

Medium/technique
Colored cement inlay

Tools & supplies
- Large sheet of paper
- Professional Grade Rapid Set Cement All
- Winsor & Newton Cotman Watercolor (I used Dioxazine violet)
- Disposable cup
- Safety glasses
- Dust mask
- Gloves
- Plastic spoons
- Pipette
- 3 empty plastic or glass containers
- Small spatula
- Toothpicks

templates (actual size)

Metal clay
- 30 grams fine-silver clay
- Paste clay
- Syringe clay with medium tip

Metal clay toolkit (p. 7)

Additional tools & supplies
- Polymer clay or two-part silicone molding compound
- Marble
- 3/8" (10mm) lock washer
- 5/16" (8mm) circle cutter
- Piece of angel hair pasta
- 2 5mm round fireable stones (I used padparadscha sapphires)
- 8" (20cm) 20-gauge sterling silver wire
- Jewelry pliers (chainnose, roundnose)
- Wire cutters
- Wire rounder or cup bur

Create the drying forms
Push a marble into a 3/4" (19mm) ball of polymer clay and remove **[A]**. Repeat to make a total of four drying forms. Bake according to the polymer clay manufacturer's instructions. (Two-part molding compound can also be used.)

Cut out and dry the flower pieces
Photocopy and cut out the flower templates. Roll 10 grams of metal clay to 3 cards/.75mm thick. Cut out one large flower and drape it on the form **[B]**. Repeat to make two large and two small flowers. Dry completely. Smooth the edges of each flower with 600-grit sandpaper.

Make the border
With a medium-tip syringe, add a clay border on the front edge of all four flower shapes **[C]**. Dry. Using syringe or paste, fill the gap between the syringe border and the base of all flowers **[D]**. Dry. Repeat until the gap is completely filled. File and sand the rough outside edges of all the flowers and the backs of the two large flowers.

Set the stones
Roll a gram of metal clay to 5 cards/1.25mm thick. Trace and cut out two lock washer shapes **[E]**. Cut a hole in the center of the clay lock washers just large enough to fit a 5mm stone (approximately 5/16"/8mm) **[F]**. Dry. Carefully file the edges of and inside each hole until the stones fit through the holes.

Add screw-head embellishments
Roll 5 grams of metal clay to 3 cards/.75mm thick. Place plastic wrap over the sheet of clay. Cut 12 circles through the plastic wrap with a 5/16" (8mm) circle cutter. Keeping the plastic wrap in place, use the back of a utility knife to press a line lightly across the surface of each circle **[G]**. Remove the plastic wrap and excess clay. Let all of the screw heads dry.

Assemble the flowers

Use a round needle file to make a hole in the center of all four flower shapes. Dry-fit the small flower, the clay lock washer, and the stone [H]. Adjust the hole in the flower until the stone sits level and below the surface of the clay lock washer. Remove the stone and paste the clay lock washer in place. Repeat this step with the other small flower and clay lock washer. Dry.

Using the medium-tip syringe, make a clay coil in the center of the large flower three passes around, avoiding the hole. Lightly press the small flower into the coil to join the two flower parts. Remove any excess clay. Dry. Repeat with the other large and small flower. Paste screw heads onto the top edge of all the large flower petals [I].

Shape the bail

Roll a gram of metal clay to 3 cards/.75mm thick. Cut two ⅛ x ⁵⁄₁₆" (3 x 8mm) strips. On the back of the large flower near an edge, paste one strip over an oiled piece of angel hair pasta [J]. Dry. Repeat on the back of the other large flower. Remove the pasta. File and sand any rough areas. You can embellish the bail with some smaller screw heads as well. Use a needle tool to scribe your name on the back, if desired.

Place the stone

Using tweezers, position the stone; it should sit just below the surface of the clay lock washer. If the fit is off, use a file to adjust the hole. No additional paste or syringe clay is necessary; the shrinkage of the clay during firing will capture and hold the stone.

Fire and add patina

Nestle the flower components in fiber blanket or vermiculite to support the petals. Fire according to the clay manufacturer's instructions. After firing, brush with a wire-bristle brush and tumble if desired. Add patina using liver of sulfur and polish as much of the patina off as you like [K]. (I added colored cement only to the lower flowers, so I left a lot of patina on the top flowers for contrast.)

Prep the cement work area

It is important to set up your work station with everything you will need for the cement application. After you start mixing the cement, you will have to work very quickly. Place a large sheet over your table to protect it. Have ready gloves, safety glasses, dust mask, a few plastic spoons and toothpicks, a container of water to rinse in, a clean cup of water to add to the cement, and a tool to mix with. Scoop about a cup of dry cement and squeeze a few paint colors onto your work surface.

Mixing and placing the cement

Fill a plastic spoon about three-quarters full of cement. Fill a pipette with clean water and add ¾ tsp. to the spoon of cement [L]. Start stirring. The cement mixture will be dry and crumbly at first, but will moisten as you continue to stir. Quickly stir in the pigment, adjusting the amount to your preference [M]. Place the flower component on the drying form. Scoop a little of the cement mixture with a toothpick and place it on a flower petal [N]. Firmly pack the cement using the edge of the toothpick [O]. Repeat until you have filled all sections on the large flower of both earrings. If cement gets onto the silver borders, wipe it off immediately. Let dry. The cement will set in just a few minutes. It will get harder the longer it sits, so drying for a few days is recommended.

Cement tips

Mixing the cement may take a few practice runs. If the cement is too crumbly, add more water. If it is too soupy, add more cement. Be aware that the paint you add also adds moisture. The workable time before the cement sets up is very short. Don't expect to fill both earrings from one mixing. I filled every other petal on both earrings first. I then mixed a second batch and filled the remaining petals; this ensured that the colors of both earrings would match.

The U-shaped end holds the earring wire in the bail and acts as the catch for the other wire end.

Make the earring wires

Cut two 4" (10cm) pieces of 20-gauge wire. Round both ends of each wire with a wire rounder or a cup bur. Use roundnose pliers to make a U bend ¼" (7mm) from one end. With chainnose pliers, bend the U shape 90 degrees as shown **[P]**. Shape the other wire in a mirror image of the first. Using the clay roller or a dowel that is about ⅞" (22mm) diameter, wrap both wires around at the same time, making sure the ends of both U bends are pointing to the side and in the direction opposite the bend **[Q]**. Use chainnose piers to make a slight bend in the straight end of both wires. String the earring wires onto the earrings **[R]**.

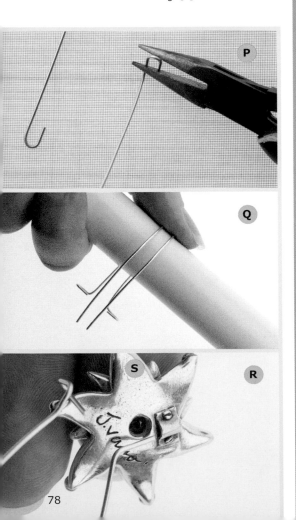

Ronna Sarvas Weltman, Three Rings, 2010. Bronze, polymer, sterling silver, resin, ancient glass, bronze heishi, shoe polish patina. Photo by Doug Yaple.

Pat Bolgar, Necklace with Leaves, 2009. Fine silver, gold-filled chain, seed beads, liver of sulfur patina. Photo by Jerry Anthony.

Window to the garden

The unusual shape of this frame requires a little extra care as you build it to be symmetrical and balanced. Much of the color in the pendant comes from the flowers and other natural items I embedded in the little window of resin, so it needed just a hint of tint. Make yours as delicate or as vibrant as you'd like.

color

Medium/technique
Items embedded in tinted resin

Tools & supplies
• UV-cure resin
• Resin dye
• Dried pressed flowers or other small items
• Clear, heavy-duty packing tape
• Toothpicks
• Index card
• UV lamp

Metal clay
• 10 grams fine-silver clay
• Syringe clay

Metal clay toolkit (p. 7)

Additional tools & supplies
• Graph paper
• Weekly pill box or other form
• 4 x 4" (10 x 10cm) glazed ceramic tile
• Large sanding swabs
• 600–2000 grit wet/dry sandpaper (optional)
• 9" (23cm) bastard file (optional)
• Metal polish (optional)

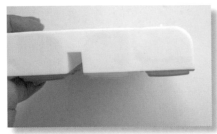

A weekly pill box made of nonstick plastic makes a great form for shaping clay. Look for one that has vertical walls, a flat bottom, and curved edges; the right shape will ensure the two clay walls fit well.

Form the frame and the bail

Oil your work surface and the bottom curve of a pill box and set aside. Condition and moisturize about 5 grams of clay. Using a nonoiled work surface, use an acrylic rolling rectangle to make a cylinder ¼" (7mm) in diameter [A]. Flatten it slightly with the roller, transfer it to the work surface, and roll it to 6 cards/1.5mm thick [B]. Trim it into a 1¾ x ⅜" (44 x 10mm) strip. Drape the strip over the edge of the pill box, making sure that one cut edge is at the beginning of the curve [C].

Make a second strip like the first. Set the pieces aside to dry on the form. After about 15 minutes, place the clay strips on a mug warmer to dry thoroughly.

From the scrap clay, make a 1 x ⅜" (26 x 10mm) strip in the same way as before. Wrap the strip around an oiled straw, overlapping the ends [D]. Trim through both layers at a 45-degree angle [E] and remove both pieces of excess clay. Apply syringe clay to the seam [F]. Press the seam together and smooth with a damp brush. Set aside to dry. Reinforce the seam if necessary and dry again.

Don't forget to oil the straw, or the bail will not come off. Wrap the clay near one end of the straw to make it easier to remove the fragile bail when it is dry.

Refine and assemble the frame

Gently sand any rough edges on the strips [G], paying special attention to the ends. Set the pieces on graph paper to be sure the walls are parallel [H]. Join the two strips, nesting the ends and applying syringe clay to the join. Dry. Reinforce the seams with syringe clay. Sand until the seams are no longer visible.

Remove the bail from the straw. Gently sand any rough edges. Sand the contact area of the bail flat to create more surface area for a better connection to the frame [I].

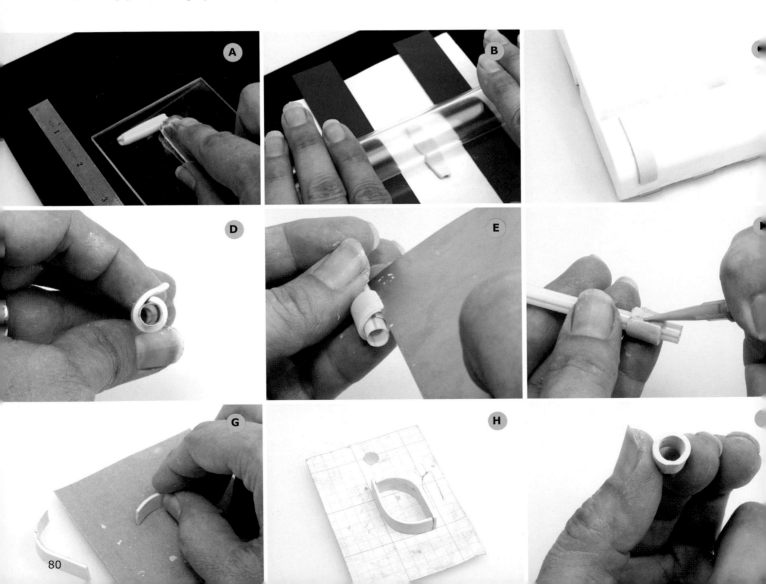

Use graph paper to center the bail on the pendant **[J]**.

> Don't trust your eyes on this one; the shape creates an optical illusion that will trick you into a lopsided pendant.

Attach the bail with syringe clay **[K]**. Dry. Add more syringe clay to form a secure connection. Dry.

Gently sand the front and back by gently moving the piece in a circular motion over a piece of sandpaper **[L]**.

Fire according to the clay manufacturer's instructions. Cool. Polish the exterior walls and the top and bottom edges. Do not polish the inside of the frame; the rough surface is easier for the resin to adhere to. Polish the interior of the bail with a sanding swab.

Apply the resin

Pull the packing tape taut, with the adhesive side up. Press the back of the pendant firmly against the tape. Burnish the tape in place **[M]**. This will prevent the resin from leaking before it is cured. Fold the ends of the tape back a bit and attach to an index card. This makes it easy to transport the assembly to and from the UV lamp.

Place a small puddle of resin and a few drops of resin dye on the tile. Add a touch of dye to the resin with a toothpick. Stir gently to avoid bubbles **[N]**. Do not use much pigment; the color will intensify as the layers build. Continue mixing until the color is even. Gently drip a 1mm thick layer of resin into the silver frame **[O]**. Coax the resin all the way to the edges with a toothpick. Cure by placing under a UV lamp for 2 minutes **[P]**. (Darker colors will take extra time to cure.)

Add another layer and cure again. Repeat until the frame is about a third full.

> To check whether the resin is cured before you add another layer, poke it gently with a toothpick. It should be firm. If not, place it under the UV lamp until it cures. For the best results, it is better to do a lot of thin layers rather than a few thick layers.

Add another shallow layer of tinted resin and use tweezers to carefully place the largest flower **[Q]**. Top with a thin layer of clear resin. Cure. Use clear resin for the remaining layers, adding objects as desired. Make sure the final layer is domed above the surface of the silver **[R]**. Cure another 4 minutes and remove the packing tape.

Optional step: Use the bastard file to file the surface of the resin flush with the

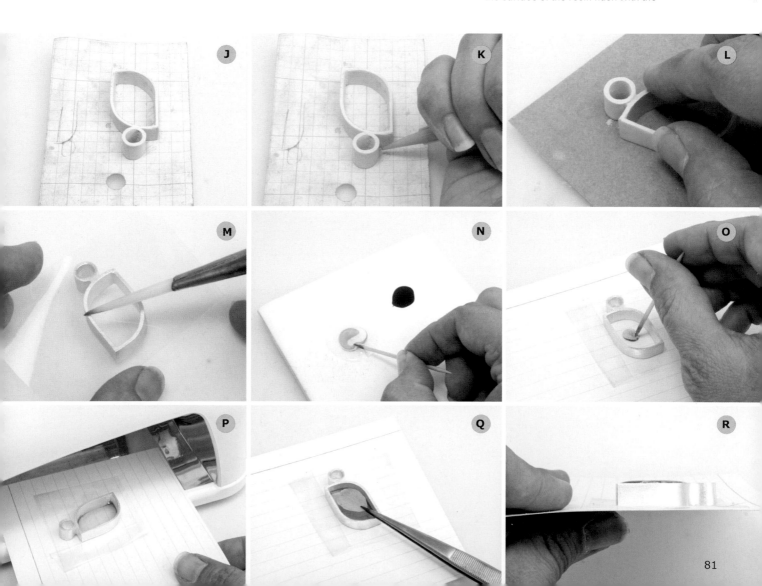

silver frame and then use damp wet/dry sandpaper to smooth the top of the resin until it is even with the top edge of the silver. Work through all the grits of the sandpaper, then wet the polishing papers and continue sanding with them.

Finally, rub the entire piece with metal polish on a soft cloth for a nice shine.

Although organic items are lovely embedded in tinted resin, you can use anything you like. I used a charm in this version.

Ann Jenkins, Red Spinner Necklace, 2011. *Fine silver, sterling silver, copper, vitreous enamel. Photo by the artist.*

Lora Hart, untitled, 2010. *Fine silver, copper, Prismacolor pencils, pearl. Photo by Drew Davidson.*

Helga Van Leipsig, Wheels, 2011. *Fine silver, sterling silver, ceramic decals. Photo by the artist.*

Hinged gems

This post earrings project combines some challenging hinge construction techniques with color provided by fireable gemstones. I used garnets, which withstand the high temperatures of firing but may shift slightly in color. You'll find many online resources that list other fireable gemstones for you to experiment with.

color

Medium/technique
Fireable gemstones

Supplies
• 2 5 x 9mm garnets

Metal clay
• 25 grams fine-silver clay
• Paste clay

Metal clay toolkit (p. 7)

Additional tools & supplies
• Texture molds
• 3 x 5" (8 x 13cm) piece of foam
• Steel pin or small T-pin
• 2 sterling earring posts
• Small metalsmith's ruler
• Jeweler's saw with a 2/0 or finer blade
• Small terra-cotta saucer
• Alumina hydrate
• 22-gauge hard sterling silver wire
• Chainnose pliers

For these earrings, I used two small molds that were complementary and worked well with the rectangular garnets. Choose your molds and make a quick sketch of the components before you get started with the clay.

Make the knuckles

The hinge will join the two components that you are molding, so the length of the hinge will be determined by the molded shapes.

For this type of hinge, you'll be making three knuckles. The two outside knuckles will be attached to the lower component and the middle knuckle will be attached to the upper component. I've set a stone in only one part of the design, but you could do this without stones or with stones on both parts (see photo on p. 86). I always make extra pieces of hinge for backup.

With an acrylic rolling rectangle, roll a small piece of metal clay into a cylinder about 2mm in diameter **[A]**. Allow the cylinder to dry to a mostly dry state. Cut the cylinder into the lengths you've determined will work for your hinges **[B]**.

Kim's hints for making hinges

The idea for these earrings came after taking a keum-boo box class with Celie Fago many years ago. Making hinges out of metal clay is a simple but exacting process. Once you make a tiny hinge out of metal clay, you'll be hooked—it's fun and challenging.

Metal clay is not as strong as metal sheet, so a little extra thought regarding structure is in order when you design metal clay jewelry piece with hinges. You'll need at least two parts to the design and a flat area for the knuckles to go.

For successful results, take time to make accurate measurements and be precise and neat while assembling the parts. Make sure the hinge you're making is long enough to support the piece.

Drill the knuckles

Using a flex shaft or a pin vise with a #65 drill bit, drill holes through the ends of the cylinders **[C]**. Let the tubes (knuckles) dry completely. If you use a mug warmer, rotate the tubes as they dry to avoid distorting them. I use a small piece of foam to support the tubes while they dry.

Drill into one side and then the other. You can usually feel if the bit is going off course and adjust the angle before it's too late.

Make the shapes

Roll the clay to 5 cards/1.25mm thick. Oil the clay and press it into the molds **[D]**. Make two top components and two bottom components. Let the pieces that will not have stones in them dry completely and file smooth. For the pieces with the stones to be set, let the pieces air dry about 5 minutes after you cut out the shape. The clay will tighten up and you'll be able to cut it without distorting the texture and shape.

Make room for the stone

Place a stone on top of the piece and locate the spot where you want to set it **[E]**. Using a craft knife, cut around the stone very

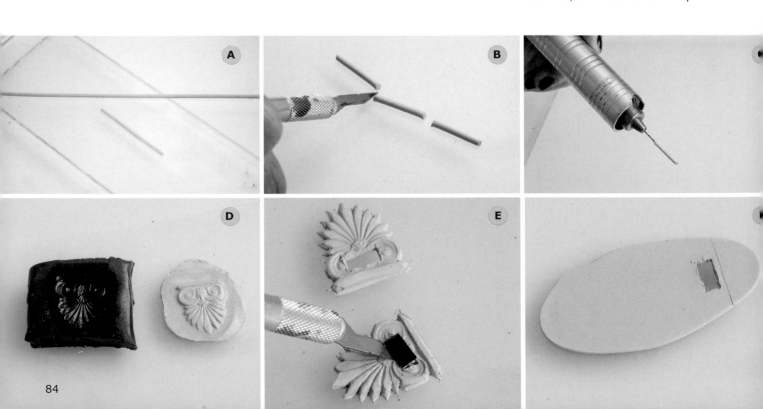

carefully, just inside the outside edge **[F]**. The hole that you are making will shrink and the stone will sit on top of it. (You can omit this step if you wish, but the hole will let light in from the back of the gem and it looks great when the earrings are worn.)

Make the bezels

Roll the excess clay to 3 cards/.75mm thick. Press the stone lightly into the clay to make an impression. Remove the stone and cut out the shape of the stone with a craft knife. Place the stone into the hole and gently press the clay closer to the stone. Don't distort the clay, but snug it into the stone a little bit. Using a tissue blade, cut around the stone leaving about a 2mm margin for the bezel **[G and H]**. Repeat for the second stone

and let the bezels dry completely. Carefully file the edges smooth. If the stone falls out, don't worry—just put it back into the bezel and let it dry completely.

Finish the edges

The bottom edge of the upper components and the top edge of the lower components must be level and straight so that the hinge will work properly. Use a file to even these edges **[I]**. Insert a T-pin (I used a steel pin from a polymer bead-making tray) through the tubes and align the top and bottom components **[J]**.

Position the earring post

Using a pencil, mark the back of each earring where its earring post will go **[K]**. Drill a small hole about .5mm deep and the diameter of

the post. My ear post has a tiny pad on it, so my holes needed to be the size of the pad.

Cut the tubes into knuckles

Measure the tubes into three equal lengths and mark them with a pencil **[L]**. Using a jeweler's saw with a 4/0 blade, carefully cut each tube into three knuckles. Try to cut the pieces perfectly straight **[M]**. I thread each knuckle set on the steel pin so I don't get them mixed up **[N]**.

Attaching knuckles and adding stones

Keeping the knuckles on the pin, put a generous amount of slip on the two outside knuckles, on only one side of the tube **[O]**.

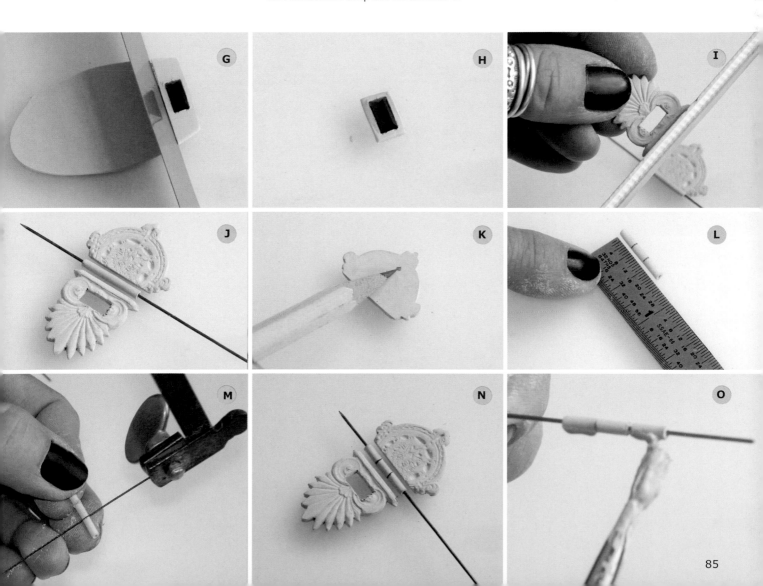

Use the same techniques to make a pair of earrings with stones in both parts.

Position the knuckles with the slip side against the top edge of the lower component and press lightly to create a good join **[P]**. Repeat for the second earring. Place the components on the foam and let them dry.

To set the bezeled stones, apply slip to the back of a bezel, making sure that it fills any gaps between the bezel and the opening in the earring component **[Q]**. Press the bezel into place. Repeat to attach the second setting to the other earring. Dry completely.

Apply some slip to the top edge of the middle knuckle **[R]**. Press it to the bottom edge of the upper component. Hold it in place **[S]** until it dries enough to put it on the foam to dry. Repeat for the other earring. Place the components on the mug warmer to dry completely.

To reinforce the middle knuckle, first remove the steel pin. Place a tiny ball of clay on the back of the upper piece where the middle knuckle is attached. Press down the ball of

clay with the edge of the craft knife blade and smear it flat around the edges **[T]**. Dry completely. Using a wet brush and/or your finger, smooth the area around the added clay. Reinsert the steel pin through the knuckles as the assembly dries **[U]**. Repeat for the other earring.

Add the ear posts
Place a small drop of water in the drilled hole for the ear post. Let it sit for a minute or two. Make a tiny ball of clay and place it on the drilled hole. Press the ear post into the ball of clay **[V]**. Use a paintbrush to smooth the area **[W]**. Repeat for the other earring.

Fire the earrings
Keeping the steel pins inserted, place the earrings into a terra-cotta saucer filled with alumina hydrate.

If a hinge gets knocked off on its way to the kiln, just scrape off the old slip, rejoin the knuckle, let it dry completely, and try again.

Fire the earrings according to the clay manufacturer's instructions.

Finish the earrings and add the hinge pin
Burnish the earrings using a drop of liquid soap and a brass-bristle brush. Tumble-polish in a rotary tumbler for about 2 hours, apply liver of sulfur patina, and polish.

Using chainnose pliers, bend a tiny L shape at the end of the 22-gauge wire. Pass the other end through the three knuckles of one earring. Use the chainnose pliers to make a tiny L at the other end of the wire and trim the excess wire. The earrings will have a lot of movement after they are hinged.

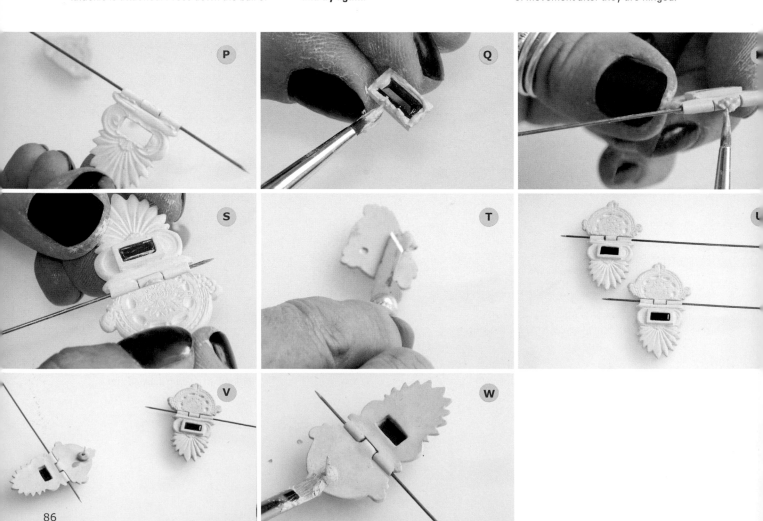

Resin window

A bright jolt of turquoise resin is the perfect "gem" for this silver clay ring. Learn how to construct a sophisticated resin reservoir using simple shapes cut from rolled clay. Then forego classic metal clay sizing issues by using a prefabricated fine-silver band paired with a decorative strap attachment.

color

Medium/technique
Tinted resin

Supplies
• Eyedropper
• Two-part resin
• Small disposable plastic container for resin
• Alcohol ink
• Wooden stir stick
• Cotton swabs
• Nail polish remover

Metal clay
• 16 grams fine-silver clay
• Thick paste clay

Metal clay toolkit (p. 7)

Additional tools & supplies
• Texture sheet
• Soft toothbrush
• Template with ovals in various sizes and degrees
• Oval doming form
• Rotary tool or flex shaft
• Brass brush attachments
• Radial bristle disks with mandrel
• 4mm-wide fine-silver ring band, ¼ size larger than desired finished size
• Unbaked scrap of polymer clay
• Metal ring mandrel and chasing hammer (optional)

Build the oval setting

Using a soft toothbrush, lightly oil a rubber texture sheet. Roll 8 grams of clay to 4 cards/1mm thick. Roll the texture sheet over the clay.

To get an accurate thickness when using a rubber texture sheet, place a texture sheet of matching thickness on either side of the clay. For example, to end up with textured clay that is 3 cards/.7mm thick, place 3 cards (or a corresponding thickness gauge) over each of the side texture sheets. Place the oiled texture sheet face down on the metal clay and roll over the clay [A].

Lightly oil an oval dome. Place a 1" (26mm) 45-degree oval template over the clay [B]. Cut out the oval shape with a needle tool or craft knife. Gently transfer the clay, design face down, onto the oval dome form [C].

Gently work the edges of the moist clay to conform to the domed shape. Dry. This is the bottom of the oval setting.

Roll the remaining clay to 4 cards/1mm and texture. Cut an oval, this time using a 1" (26mm) 60-degree oval. Carefully center a ¾" (19mm) 30-degree oval over the large oval and cut an opening. Form this oval ring on the same (or duplicate) doming form, design face up, to dry [D]. This is the top of the setting.

Place the back oval face down on a piece of 300-grit sandpaper. Move gently in a figure-8 pattern to remove the raised edge [E]. This creates a small bevel around the edges so that the bottom oval will fit within the top oval. Smooth and refine the inner and outer edges of the top oval [F].

Moisten the beveled edge of the bottom

oval and the back of the top oval with water. Apply a small amount of thick paste around the beveled edge with a brush or clay shaper. Working from the back, tightly fit the bottom oval into the top oval. Use a soft clay shaper to fill and smooth the seam. This attachment needs to be secure to prevent leakage of resin later [G]. Dry.

Attach the ring shank

To improve attachment to the ring shank, lightly file a texture onto a ¼" (7mm) wide area on the outside of the band [H].

The strap used to attach the band will make the ring about a quarter size smaller than the loose band.

Roll the remaining clay to 3 cards/.75mm thick and cut a ¾" (19mm) 45-degree oval. Moisten the back of the oval setting and add the new oval of wet clay, pressing

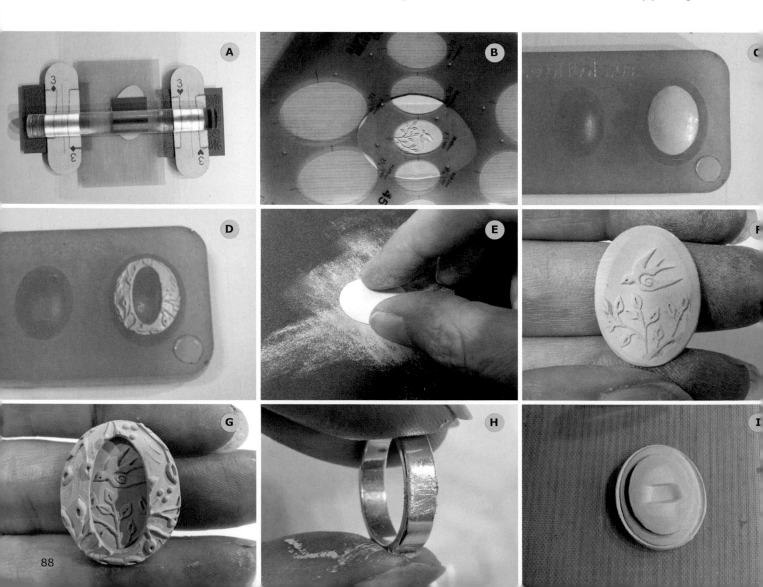

the edges down gently to conform to the curvature. While the clay is still wet, press the ring shank into the moist clay to indent the attachment point and remove **[I]**. Dry the setting. Refine the edge by sanding and polishing.

Roll the remaining clay and texture as before. Then use a ¾" 30-degree oval to cut a final oval. This oval strap will attach the ring shank to the oval setting. Center and drape the strap over the ring shank **[J]**. Dry the pieces together. Remove the shank and refine the edges of the strap.

Apply thick paste to the back of the oval setting where the shank will attach, then center the ring shank with the roughened area in contact with the paste **[K]**.

Add more thick paste or fresh clay to fill the areas on the top oval on either side of the shank. Place the oval strap over the metal band **[L]**. Dry.

Fill gaps on either side of the attachment with fresh clay, not paste (paste shrinks more than clay) **[M]**. Use a soft clay shaper to smooth and blend the sides of the attachment points **[N]**. Dry and then refine all of the exposed clay with polishing pads.

Finish the ring
To support the ring during firing, embed the shank in a bowl of vermiculite so the oval setting is fully supported **[O]**. Fire according to the clay manufacturer's instructions. For standard fine-silver clay, fire for 2 hours (rings benefit from the maximum strength created by the long firing).

Burnish the ring with a brass-bristle brush. I use a brass brush attachment in a rotary tool for fast progress **[P]**. Support the ring on a rubber block as needed.

Vary the size and shape of the brass brush attachments to access tight spots like the inside of the resin setting or inner wall of the shank.

Fill the bezel with resin
To support the ring while you pour the resin, adhere a ball of unbaked polymer clay to your work surface and press the ring into the clay **[Q]**. Make sure the reservoir is level so that resin won't flow over the edge.

To test the level as well as the color, add a few drops of alcohol ink to a dish of water (You can blend custom colors of the ink if you wish.) Use an eyedropper to fill the reservoir in the oval setting **[R]**. Adjust the ring position as needed so that the liquid is level all around the perimeter. Remove the water with the dropper (a cotton swab or

small sponge can collect wayward fluid) and let the reservoir air dry.

Using a small plastic container, carefully measure equal volumes of both resin and hardener. A syringe-style dual dispenser makes this easy for small volumes, such as the quarter ounce I used **[S]**.

Add a drop of alcohol ink and mix slowly with a wooden stir stick to combine the resin components. Introduce as few bubbles as possible. If desired, add one or two more drops of ink for more intense color. Scrape the bottom and sides, mixing for at least 2 minutes. Let rest for 5 minutes to allow air bubbles to escape.

Carefully pour the colored resin into the reservoir **[T]**. It is better to underfill because the resin may expand slightly as it cures. If any resin escapes the reservoir, clean it with a cotton swab dipped in nail polish remover.

Place the reservoir under a desk lamp to gently warm bubbles and allow them to release more easily. Do not heat more aggressively to avoid damage to the resin.

Check after 10 minutes or so for bubbles, which may need to be teased free with a needle. Let the resin set undisturbed **[U]**; cover the ring to protect the resin from dust overnight. Don't throw the excess resin away; set it aside and the next day, touch a toothpick to the surface to verify that the resin has cured.

Never touch the resin surface of the jewelry piece until testing the remainder shows it is fully hardened. No fingerprints allowed!

Adding patina
Heat a small amount of water to near boiling, then add a brush full of liver of sulfur gel. Use a brush to apply the patina only to the areas where some extra definition will be an accent, such as the textured areas on the front and back **[V]**.

Do not submerge the resin in the patina; it may discolor.

After the patina has darkened the metal, rinse the ring in fresh water and baking soda. Remove excess patina with radial bristle disks in a rotary tool: Mount three

or more disks on a mandrel so that the long, curved abrasive fingers fold back with the spin, not against it **[W]**. Avoiding the resin, carefully remove patina from the darkened areas. The 80-grit disks will leave a matte finish on the silver. If a shiny finish is preferred, use higher grits.

Try the ring on to check sizing. A ring mandrel won't give an accurate size because the opening is not circular. If the ring is too snug, slide the ring onto a ring mandrel and tap the back side of the shank repeatedly with a chasing hammer to both work-harden and enlarge the ring **[X]**.

To remove tarnish and shine to raised areas, polish with a polishing cloth.

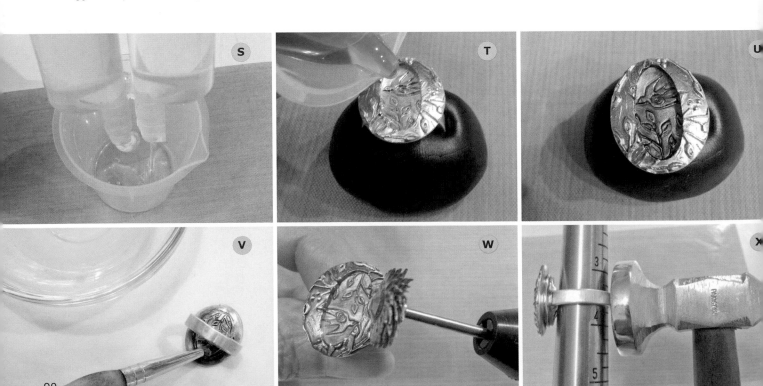

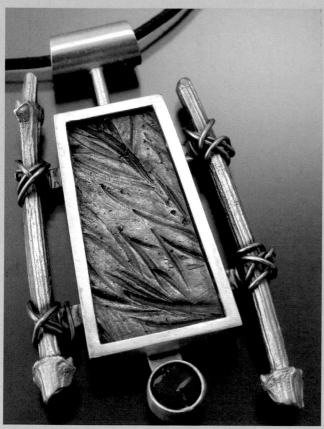

Michael Thee, Autumn Spruce, 2011. *Sterling silver, bronze, Madeira citrine, liver of sulfur patina.*

Lorena Angulo, Veronica's Necklace, 2009. *Fine silver, bronze, photos, resin, pearls, sterling silver wire, copper wire. Photo by George Post.*

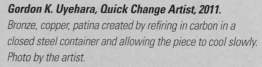

Gordon K. Uyehara, Quick Change Artist, 2011. *Bronze, copper, patina created by refiring in carbon in a closed steel container and allowing the piece to cool slowly. Photo by the artist.*

Hadar Jacobson, Gradient Scene, 2011. *Copper, bronze, steel, white bronze.*

Enamel illusions

In this project, you'll learn a fresh technique for making a polymer clay mold, and then use it to create a metal clay pendant with textured, recessed areas to hold color and resin. This method produces a fantastic imitation of transparent vitreous enamel. I often create spacer beads to accent my pendants in the same way.

color

Technique/medium
Resin with gold leaf and alcohol ink

Tools & supplies
- ⅛ sheet 23K patent or loose gold leaf
- ¼" (7mm) square 23.5k gold foil
- 1mm diamond-ball bur and battery-operated engraver or flex shaft
- UV-cure resin
- UV lamp
- #0 round paintbrush
- Isopropyl alcohol
- Cosmetic sponges
- Butane lighter
- Tweezers
- Alcohol inks
- Permanent blender marker
- Wet/dry sandpaper with white backing such as 3M Imperial Micro-Finishing Film (30, 15, and 9 micron)
- 3M Tri-M-Ite polishing papers (1200, 4000, 6000, and 8000 grit)
- Finishing UV resin such as ibd Intense Seal

Template (actual size)

Metal clay
• 25 grams fine-silver clay

Metal clay toolkit (p. 7)

Additional tools & supplies
• 4 oz. Sculpey Mold Maker
• Sculpey Translucent Liquid
• Cosmetic sponge
• Isopropyl alcohol
• Ball stylus
• Ceramic tile
• Pasta machine
• Craft oven

Design the pendant shape

The black lines of the design template represent the high silver walls of the finished pendant. The open white areas of the design represent the recessed cells that you'll later fill with resin (see photo I on p. 94). Make two photocopies of the **template**.

Transfer the image to make the mold

Condition 2 oz. of Sculpey Mold Maker and run through the pasta machine on a medium-thick setting. Lay the polymer clay sheet on a ceramic tile. Place the image face down on the polymer. Wet a cosmetic sponge with isopropyl alcohol and blot the back of the paper, being careful not to let the paper shift **[A]**.

Lift a corner of the paper to see if the toner has transferred. If it hasn't, blot it with more isopropyl alcohol. When the image has transferred, remove the paper. You don't need a perfect transfer because it will be used only as a cutting guide.

Spritz the polymer with water. Texture the areas inside the black lines with a ball stylus **[B]**.

Cut along both sides of each black line with a craft knife. Hold the blade straight down so the cuts won't be angled **[C]**.

Carefully remove the cut polymer **[D]**. If a piece doesn't want to lift out cleanly, leave it there rather than risk smudging other areas. It can be removed with a craft knife after the polymer has been baked. Bake according to the manufacturer's instructions. Let the polymer cool completely before you remove the pieces from the tile.

Place another sheet of Mold Maker on the tile and transfer the same image as before. Smear a light layer of Sculpey Translucent Liquid over the transferred image. Position the baked pieces on the unbaked clay using the image transfer as a guide **[E]**. Trim excess clay and bake again to cure **[F]**.

Make the silver clay pendant

Thoroughly oil the mold. Flatten 25 grams of silver clay so it's slightly larger than the mold's impression and press it into the mold **[G]**. Texture the back of the clay if desired. Lift the piece **[H]** and place it on a flat

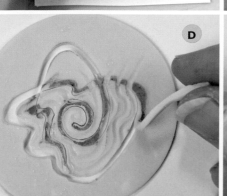

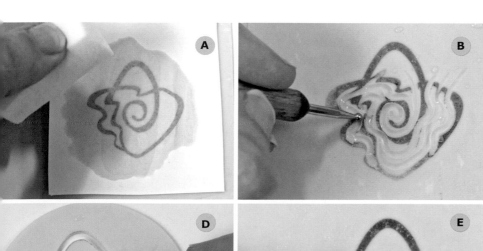

surface. Trim and store the excess clay. Let the silver piece dry.

Wait to cut out the inside of the bail until you finish other sanding and finishing. After that area is removed, the bail will be vulnerable to breakage.

The recessed areas can be carved and fine-tuned with a 1.5mm U-gouge tool. After the usual sanding and finishing, a shallow texture can be carved into the side and top walls with a V-gouge tool.

Fire the pendant according to the metal clay manufacturer's instructions. Brush the piece with a brass brush and soapy water. Tumble and polish for a bright shine **[I]**.

Prepare the surface for color

Texture the areas that will receive color with an engraver tool or flex-shaft and a 1mm diamond ball bur **[J]**. Rotate the metal while texturing, so that the light catches the metal from different directions.

Using UV resin as a clear primer over textured metal makes subsequent colors brighter. UV resin has several advantages: It's crystal clear, adheres to the metal, bubbles are easy to remove, and best of all, it cures in a few minutes under a UV lamp.

Warm the UV resin on a mug warmer. Clean the pendant with a cosmetic sponge dipped in isopropyl alcohol to remove silver dust that settled during texturing **[K]**. Use a #0 round paintbrush to apply a thin layer of warm resin to every area that will receive color. Pop bubbles with a butane lighter **[L]**. Any lint can be removed with tweezers.

Remove excess resin from the areas that will not be colored. I use a pointed-tip permanent blender marker filled with clear isopropyl alcohol. (To remove the resin from the marker tip, wipe it on a piece of scrap paper.) Cure the resin under a UV lamp for about 3 minutes, and then use a cosmetic sponge dipped in isopropyl alcohol to wipe away the sticky layer that you'll find on top of the cured resin.

Add gold

Enamelists often fire transparent enamels over gold foil. It looks fabulous under resin too. Transparent green, yellow, and red are especially brilliant when placed over gold.

Paint a light layer of resin only in the areas where you want to add gold. Lay a sheet of gold leaf face down on those areas, press, and it will easily transfer **[M]**. Or, pick up a little gold with a clay shaper and mix it into the resin **[N]**.

Cure the resin for 3 minutes. Don't wipe off the sticky top layer. Instead, add a bit more resin to cover the gold. Cure again and wipe with alcohol.

Add color

Color the resin with one or a few colors of alcohol ink **[O]**. If you don't like what you've done, you can erase some or all of it with the blender marker or isopropyl alcohol and start over. You haven't committed to the color until you cure more resin on top of it.

When your first layer of color is done, apply a layer of UV resin and cure for 3 minutes. UV resin needs longer to cure when put over darker colors, so with each layer, I like to give the piece a little more time under the UV lamp. Testing with resin over a specific color on a spare piece of aluminum can help you determine how long it needs for curing.

Add another layer or two of color, following each with a layer of resin **[P]**. Each time you add resin, be sure to pop the bubbles and remove excess resin from the higher silver

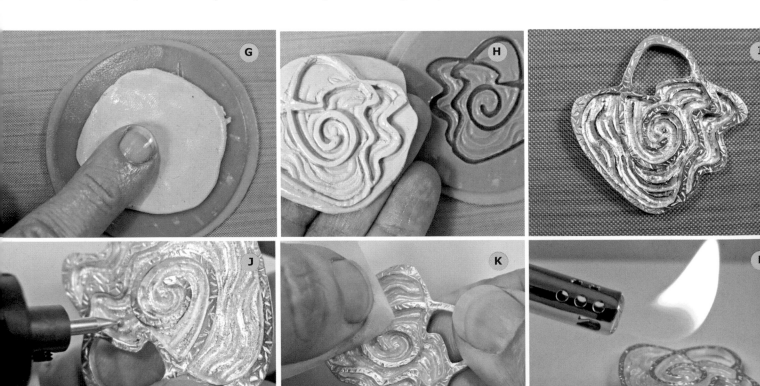

Simulating enamel layers

Enamelists use layers of transparent colors of powdered glass to build vibrant depth. You can create an equally spirited depth of color with layers of transparent ink and resin. After experimenting with numerous types of paint, I concluded that alcohol inks are the best choice for a glass-like transparency on resin. There are several brands of alcohol inks on the market. My hands-down favorite are the Copic markers for their smooth application, wide color selection, and refillable product design.

You can apply the color in a few different ways. Most of the time, I color the metal directly with a marker, but you can also apply the marker or bottle ink to a palette and use a brush and isopropyl alcohol as you would with watercolors.

Because you are working with transparent colors, each layer of color will blend with the colors under it to create a richer and darker color. For example, if you color a layer with yellow, then put magenta in the next layer, they will merge to produce a bright red. For this reason, start with lighter colors and be aware that if warm and cool colors are layered on top of each other, they will mix to create darker, muted colors. And, if you want the end product to have a pure hue or specific color, every layer must work together to achieve it.

level with a blender marker before curing. When the layers of resin have reached nearly the same height as the top level of silver, you can choose to stop there, so that the higher silver isn't covered with resin. Or you can continue to add resin and it will create a natural dome over the entire area.

Using scissors, cut three small squares of 23.5k gold foil between two sheets of tracing paper. Gold foil is thicker than gold leaf, so it will stay in one piece while you apply it. Remove the paper and stick the foil on the pendant with a dot of resin [Q]. Cure. Follow with an entire layer of resin to fully cover the foil and evenly add to the entire dome of resin.

Sand the piece

After adding numerous layers, the dome of resin might be lumpy in areas. UV resin can be sanded with wet/dry sandpaper. Use a white sandpaper because black sandpaper will leave a black residue on the resin. Start with a wet square of 400-grit paper to shape the dome, then progress to finer grits [R].

When you start sanding, the resin will become cloudy, but as you move to the finer grits, you will start to see the shine come back. Occasionally wiping the piece with isopropyl alcohol will remind you how beautiful the finished piece will be.

To bring the resin to a full shine, you can wipe it with a metal polish such as Wenol. An alternative product for a final, glassy topcoat is called ibd Intense Seal. It also cures under the UV light, but doesn't leave a sticky top layer.

If the resin needs to be removed from the silver, soak it in acetone for a couple of hours. Another product that works quickly, Attack Adhesive Remover, is formulated to dissolve cured epoxy, cyanoacrylates, and polyester resins. Neither product will harm the silver.

Lora Hart, untitled, 2010. *Fine silver, sterling silver, Faux Bone, felt, brass, silk, glass. Photo by Drew Davidson.*

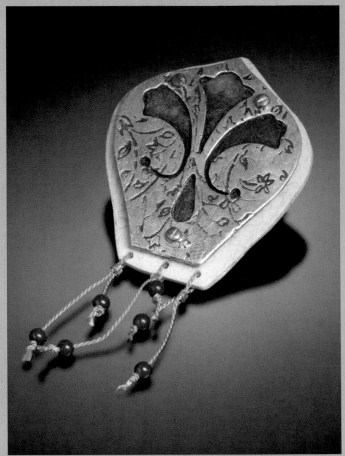

Pat Bolgar, Brooch #3, 2009. *Fine silver, polymer. Photo by Jerry Anthony.*

Liz Hall, Eyecon, 2012. *Fine silver, sterling silver, polymer clay, iridescent media, resin. Photo by the artist.*

Enameled riverbed

Fired enamel has a rich, jewel-like clarity and depth that no other medium can achieve. In this project, you'll learn how to inset enamel into textured copper clay. Tiny pieces of foil below the transparent surface create an intriguing pattern and intensify the color and sense of depth.

color

Technique/medium
Enamel

Tools & supplies
- Thompson lead-free enamels: LCE-1 Black (powder form), 1995 Black, 2410 Copper Green, 2420 Sea Green, 2430 Beryl Green, 2435 Turquoise
- Fine silver enameling foil
- PennyBrite
- Toothbrush
- Ammonia
- Fiberglass scratch brush
- Very fine-tip round paintbrushes
- Scribe or awl
- Enamel spatula
- Tweezers
- Scissors
- Distilled water
- Klyr-Fire enamel adhesive with sprayer
- Enameling trivet with rack
- Firing fork
- 200-mesh screen with two caps
- 40-mesh medium sifter
- N100 dust mask
- Alundum stone or diamond sanding stick
- Wet/dry sandpaper, various grits

Copper clay quirks

Copper clay has a few quirks that make working with it a little different than working with silver clay. It can be very hard right out of the package and may need to be conditioned; rolling it out inside a plastic report cover a few times will soften it up without drying it out. Copper clay does not adhere to itself as easily as silver. Reinforce all joins and seams with extra clay to prevent them from coming apart when firing.

Metal clay
• 20–30 grams copper clay

Metal clay toolkit (p. 7)

Additional tools & supplies
• 8mm embeddable copper bail
• 2 2.5mm copper eyelets
• Copper jump rings
• Thin cardboard
• Pickle (Sparex)
• Liver of sulfur

Make the copper clay base
Adhere a piece of clear plastic packing tape to the thin cardboard backing from a notepad and cut a mask the size and shape you want your enamel inset. The packing tape will prevent the clay from sticking to the porous cardboard [A].

Stack thickness gauges on either side of a texture stamp to create a platform for rolling the clay to 16 cards/4mm thick. The roller should sit 1.25–1.5mm (5–6 cards) above the surface of the texture when sitting on the slats or cards.

Apply a thin coat of release agent to the taped side of the cardboard mask piece and the texture mat. Position the mask on the texture, tape side up, noting the direction you want it in relationship to the design.

Condition the copper clay and roll it to 7 cards/1.75mm thick on a nonstick work surface. Place it over the texture and mask. Starting in the middle, firmly run the roller up and back in the long direction of the mask. Remove the clay from the texture and peel the mask out of the clay. The smooth inset area should be crisply defined [B].

Use a shape template and a needle tool to cut out the piece [C]. Dry completely.

To make the bail bar, roll a strip of clay to 10 cards/2.5mm thick. Cut a rectangle approximately ¼" (7mm) wide and as long as the width of your piece. Insert the embeddable copper bail in the center top [D]. Insert a copper eyelet on each side of the bottom. Dry completely.

Dampen the clay around the embeddable bail and eyelets and use very moist clay and a rubber clay shaper to reinforce the base of each inserted piece [E]. Use a damp flat brush to smooth the additional clay into the existing clay to create a seamless join. Check the inset area on the pendant to ensure the edges are crisp and sharp and that there are no bits of overhanging clay. To make adjustments, dampen the clay first and use a small file or a clay cleanup tool [F]. Dry, sand, and smooth the edges of both pieces.

The final step before firing is to drill holes for jump rings on each side of the top of the textured piece to join it to the bail. Keep in mind the clay will shrink anywhere from 12–20%, depending on the brand. The holes need to easily accommodate a 16-gauge jump ring after firing.

Align the eyelets with the textured piece and mark where the holes will go. Use a pin vise and drill bits to drill the holes. Create a

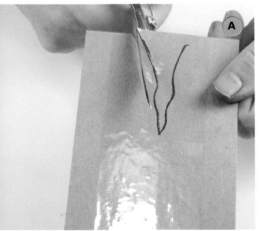

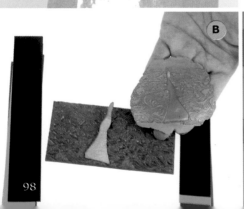

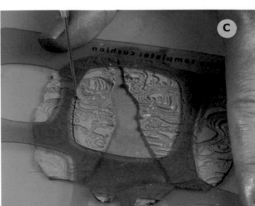

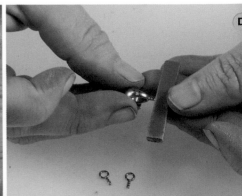

pilot hole with a small bit before drilling with a larger bit.

Fire the base
Your firing method will depend on the type of clay you use. Art Clay Copper is fired on an open shelf without carbon. COPPRclay requires a two-phase firing schedule in order to enamel properly.

Firing an Art Clay Copper piece
Remove the kiln shelf and pre-heat the kiln to 1780°F (971°C). Nest the piece between two thin layers of fiber blanket on a piece of fiber paper on the shelf **[G]**. Use very long tongs and a heat-resistant glove to place the shelf in the kiln. Fire for 35 minutes.

As quickly as safely possible, remove the shelf from the kiln and dump the pieces, fiber blanket, metal clay, and fiber paper into a bucket of water. The majority of the firescale will stick to the fiber blanket and not your piece. Quenching the hot piece will usually cause a piece to warp. Place the piece face down in a gently domed dapping block and use a wooden punch to reshape the piece into a nice curve **[H]**. Dapping will usually remove any remaining firescale; however, if there is still stubborn scale, you can place the piece in hot pickle solution

such as Sparex for 15–30 minutes.

Firing a COPPRclay piece
For a COPPRclay piece, use the following two-phase firing schedule. Do not put COPPRclay in pickle solution under any circumstances—it will destroy the enamel you apply later.

Phase 1: Binder burnout
Place the piece on an open shelf in a cold kiln. Fire at Ramp Speed 500°F (260°C) per hour to a temperature of 560°F (293°). Hold for 15 minutes. At the end of phase 1, the piece will be black and brittle. Handle with care.

Phase 2: Sintering
Place 1" (26mm) of carbon in a firing pan. Place the piece face down and cover with another ½" (13mm) of carbon. Place the lid on the pan. Fire at Ramp Speed Full to a temperature of 1780°F (971°C). Hold for 3.5 hours. Allow the piece to cool completely in the carbon.

Prepare the enamel powders
Sizing transparent enamels using screens will greatly improve its clarity. The following steps should be used for all the enamels listed for this project EXCEPT LCE-1 Black

and 1995 Black, which are opaque and should be used unscreened.

Wear an N100 dust mask while screening your enamels. Place a 200-mesh screen in a plastic lid. Place enamel and a coin in the screen and put another plastic lid on top. Shake the stack back and forth to screen out the fine particles. The coin will help push the enamel through the screen. Use the enamel remaining on top of the screen, not what was sifted out. Discard the enamel that ends up in the lid.

Put the screened enamel into a plastic spoon, and use a permanent marker to label the color on the handle. Add some distilled water to the enamel and agitate it gently with the enamel spatula. Pour off the excess water. This will remove any remaining fine particles and prepare the enamel for use.

Prepare the LCE-1 for use by mixing a small amount of the powder with just enough distilled water to give it the consistency of heavy cream.

Prepare the metal for enameling
Soak the metal piece for five minutes in a solution of two parts very hot water and one part clear ammonia to neutralize acidity

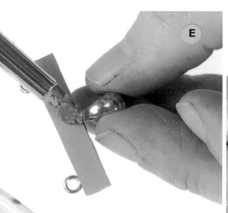

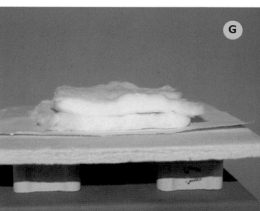

Counter-enamel and flux

Counter-enamel is enamel that's applied to the back of a piece. For copper, this serves two purposes: It will help prevent cracks in the enamel on the front of the piece and will protect the back from firescale and oxidation.

In enameling, "flux" refers to the first layer of enamel that is applied to the front of a piece and is either clear or a very pale color. Dark or medium colors applied directly to copper become very dark. Flux is necessary to keep the colors vivid. If copper is fired at too low a temperature or not long enough, it will oxidize and take on a dark reddish or mottled look. After firing, the copper should appear clean and bright through the enamel.

In order to avoid firescale forming on any of the areas to be enameled, both the counter-enamel and the flux should be applied and fired at the same time.

from the burned out binders, carbon, or the pickle. Rinse and then tumble for a minimum of 2 hours.

Clean the metal piece with a glass brush and ammonia. The water should sheet off the metal rather than beading up. Beading is caused by oils on the surface which could prevent the enamel from adhering correctly. Dry the piece with a paper towel and take care not to touch the areas to be enameled with your fingers.

Apply the counter-enamel
Preheat the kiln to 1550°F (843°C). Place the metal piece on a trivet. Paint a thin coat of LCE-1 onto the back of the piece **[I]**. While the LCE is still wet, use the sifter to apply a layer of dry 1995 Black enamel **[J]**. The LCE should be completely covered, but the enamel should not be mounded. Lightly mist Klyr-Fire over the piece. Don't spray directly at the enamel **[K]**. The counter-enamel should form a crust on the piece that will not drop off when you turn it over. Place the piece face up in the trivet. Use a damp brush to remove any black enamel from the front of the piece and the jump ring holes.

Apply the flux (first coat of enamel)
Use 2410 Copper Green for the flux coat. The enamel should be very wet. A brush should pass easily through the enamel, not glide over the top. Fill the entire inset by picking up small amounts of enamel with the brush, and pushing the enamel onto the piece with the scribe **[L]**. If the enamel does not apply easily to the piece, it is probably too dry; add a bit more water. Cover the metal completely but not too thickly.

Too little enamel will result in firescale forming in the bare spots and marring the piece. Too much will fill the space too quickly and not leave enough room for color shading.

After the entire area is filled, gently tap the edge of the piece with a tool handle to settle and smooth the enamel and bring the water to the surface **[M]**. Touch a piece of paper

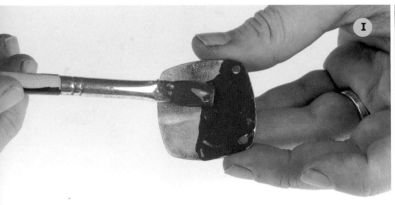

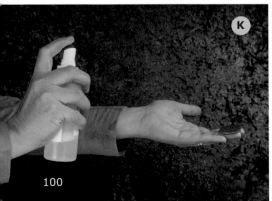

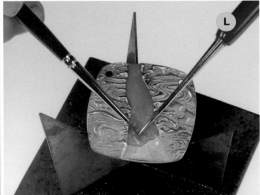

towel to the edge of the enamel to draw off the excess water **[N]**. Use a magnifier to carefully check for grains of enamel on the textured areas of the piece. Use a damp brush to remove them. With the piece still on the trivet, place it on top of the kiln to dry.

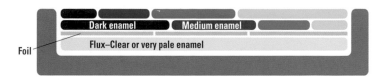

Figure

Fire the enamel
Use a firing fork to place the trivet in the preheated kiln **[O]**. Fire for approximately 2 minutes, until the enamel is smooth and glossy and the copper is clean and bright under the enamel. If the copper under the enamel is dark when you check it, return it to the kiln for another minute. Timing of enamels begins from the moment you close the door of the kiln.

As the piece cools, firescale will form on the exposed copper. You may hear a crackling sound and bits of scale may pop off **[P]**. This is normal.

After the piece is cool, scrub the piece with hot water, PennyBrite, and a toothbrush to remove the firescale **[Q]**. Only the loose scale needs to be removed so that it does not come off during firing and mar your enamels; it's not necessary to remove all the scale at this point.

After you have successfully fired the flux coat, lower the kiln temperature to 1450°F (788°C). All remaining enamel firing will be done at this temperature.

Apply the foil
Fine-silver foil will add sparkle to the enamel. Cut the foil into small strips. Dip a brush in Klyr-Fire and use it to pick up and position the bits of foil on the enamel. You can also use the tweezers or the scribe to help with positioning **[R]**. Set the piece on the kiln to dry. Fire at 1450°F (788°C) for 1–1½ minutes to fuse the foil to the enamel.

Enamel shading
You can create depth and shading by layering the enamel. Using a very fine-tip paintbrush and a scribe, pick up small amounts of enamel and apply them to the enamel inset area. Working your way from the bottom to the top, apply each color in a deep V, starting with 2435 Turquoise and moving on to 2430 Beryl, 2420 Sea Green,

and 2410 Copper Green until the entire area has been covered with a thin layer of enamel. Use the scribe to mix the grains a bit where the colors come together **[S]**.

Tap the edge of the piece to settle the enamel and bring the water to the surface. Wick away excess water with a paper towel. Use a damp brush to remove any stray grains. Dry and fire for 1½–2 minutes, until the enamel is smooth and glossy. Cool the piece. Remove firescale by scrubbing with PennyBrite, hot water, and a toothbrush.

Apply the enamel colors as before, but do not extend the turquoise quite as far up. Overlap the darker colors with the next-lighter color **[figure]**.

Finishing
Clean off as much firescale as you can by scrubbing. If enamel got on the edge of the piece, use water and an alundum stone to

Red, orange, and yellow enamels react negatively with silver foil, so use gold enameling foil to create this look. My enamel colors were 2880 Woodrow Red, 2850 Sunset Orange, 2840 Mandarin Orange, and 2215 Egg Yellow.

grind it off **[T]**. Wet/dry sandpaper can be used to remove the scratches from the grinding. Remember, all grinding and sanding must be done wet when working with enamels.

Tumble the piece for 30–60 minutes to return the copper to a shiny and burnished condition. Tumbling will not harm the enamel. If desired, apply a liver of sulfur patina to provide definition to the textured area. Join the piece to the bail using 16-gauge jump rings **[U]**.

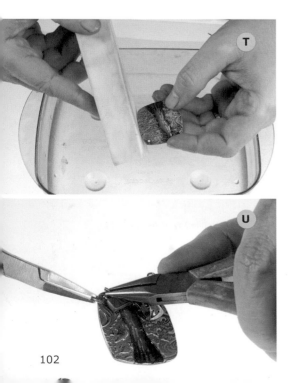

Cindy Silas, Promenade, 2008. *Fine silver, polymer, acrylic. Photo by Jerry Anthony.*

Sue Urquhart, Burning Love, 2012. *Fine silver, tinted concrete. Photo by the artist.*

DESIGNER **Lorrene Baum-Davis**

Legends rings

This ring project, part of what I call my Legends series of rings, signifies the end of an artistic slump I experienced after the 2008 passing of my dear husband, Phil. You'll use advanced metal clay skills and learn how to slump glass in a kiln to create the curved cabochon. Plan to devote three days to this project.

color

Technique/medium
Fused glass

Tools & supplies
- Glass (Bullseye COE 90): scraps of 2mm thick black, 2mm thick transparent dichroic, 3mm thick clear cap glass
- Glass coldworking tools
- Bowl of water
- Safety glasses
- 1¾ " x ½" (44 x 13mm) diamond flat file
- Diamond sanding pads (60-grit optional)
- Good-quality lighting

Metal clay
- 40 grams fine-silver clay
- Syringe clay
- Paste clay
- Art Clay Silver Overlay Paste

Metal clay toolkit (p. 7)

Additional tools & supplies
- Ceramic clay
- Ring shank guide
- Cotton swab
- Isopropyl alcohol
- Tuna can filled with silica sand or 2" (51mm) square thick fiber blanket
- Kiln furniture: 4 short stilts
- Kiln shelf coated with kiln wash

Firing ceramics

Stoneware traditionally gets fired at cone 09 (1683°F/917°C), which creates a durable form. To save time, we'll fire the ceramic form at the same time we fuse the glass. Please handle this form with care because it will not have been fired at the most desirable temperature for the optimum length of time. Consult a ceramics book and/or talk to your clay supplier for additional firing schedules for other ceramic products.

DAY 1

Make the ceramic slumping form

Coat the kiln shelf with kiln wash and let dry. Pinch off a golfball-size lump of ceramic clay and roll it to 8 cards/2mm thick in a long oval. Trim it to about 1½ x 6" (38mm x 15cm) **[A]**. Cover a ¾" (19mm) diameter marker with plastic wrap and wrap the clay over it in a smooth, even U shape. Prop the marker with the clay on top **[B]**. Let the form partially dry and remove the marker. Place the clay in a toaster oven or a dehydrator set to 200°F (93°C) for a minimum of 2 hours.

Using coarse sandpaper or sheetrock sanding strips, sand the edges of the form so they are flat **[C]**. Smooth the top and sides. Place the form on the kiln shelf.

Fuse the glass cabochon

Cut the black and dichroic glass scraps to ½ x ¾" (12 x 20mm). Cut the cap glass to ¾ x 1" (20 x 24mm). Carefully clean the glass with isopropyl alcohol and wipe dry. Stack with the black on the bottom, dichroic face up, and the cap glass on top. Place the stack on the kiln shelf opposite the ceramic form **[D]**.

The initial fuse

These guidelines are for fusing small objects. Every kiln is different; adjust your firing temperatures accordingly.

If your kiln has a vent with a plug, keep the vent open until the temperature reaches 800°F (427°C) to release any water left in the ceramic clay body. Although the clay may feel dry, it contains some water. (It's OK if your kiln has no plug.)

Suggested schedule

- Unplug the vent: R1 500°F (260°C) per hour to 800°F (427°C), hold 15 minutes
- Plug the vent: R2 AFAP to 1450°F (788°C), hold 10 minutes
- R3 AFAP to 960°F (516°C)
- R4: Off

Ramp = R; AFAP = As Fast As Possible

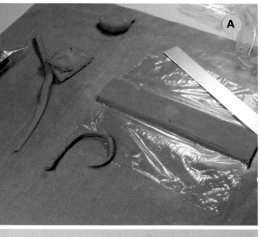

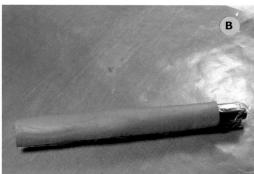

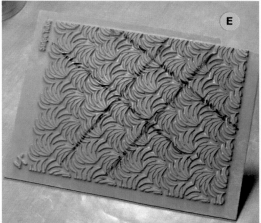

Cool the kiln completely to room temperature. If the glass cools too quickly, thermal shock may cause the clay or glass to crack and be unstable.

I have a Paragon SC2 kiln. These schedules work in my kiln, but remember to adjust for yours.

Create the ring shank
Use permanent marker to mark the area of the texture sheet you'd like to use **[E]**. Copy the ring template or draw a box. (The mark will come off later with regular use or rubbing alcohol.)

Lightly oil the plastic sheet and the parchment or nonstick paper. Use a paintbrush to lightly oil the texture sheet, making sure you get into all the nooks and crannies.

Wrap the ring mandrel in nonstick paper strips. Tape the ends of the paper together, but not to the mandrel; later you'll slide off the ring shank and paper together.

On parchment or nonstick paper, roll about 10 grams of metal clay to 8 cards/2mm thick about 9 x 60mm. Place the clay sheet on the marked texture sheet, place 6-card/1.5mm

thickness gauges on each side, cover with divider plastic, and roll over the clay to texture it **[F]**.

Using a ring shank guide, trim to the desired length and width (no wider than 9mm) **[G]**.

Make the ring about 1½ sizes larger than the desired finished size. (Adjust this number based on the brand of clay you're using and your experience.)

The lines marked "GUIDE" on the ring shank guide indicate the size that the ring shank will be after firing.

Use a mister to moisten the textured clay strip. Carefully drape the strip around the nonstick paper on the mandrel, supporting the base so the shank will not stretch.

Allow a bit of an overlap at the join and smear the clay over the ring strip **[H]**. This will give the inside of the shank a smooth surface that will need very little finishing with sanding tools. Wrap the opposite end around the ring strip and gently smear that end into the clay. This join will be hidden by the glass cab.

Trim the excess clay from the shank **[I]**. Smooth the join again. Leave the shank on the mandrel to dry on a mug warmer or in a dehydrator.

When the clay is medium dry, slip it off the mandrel, keeping it on the parchment or nonstick paper. (If it dries completely, it can be difficult to remove the shank without breaking it.) Dry a bit longer, remove the parchment/nonstick paper, and then dry completely.

Use a pencil to mark a line along the widest and narrowest part of the shank. Place 220-grit sandpaper on the work surface and gently sand the open edges using a figure-8 motion. The goal is to make the shank narrower on the bottom, so gently hold your fingers close to the bottom as you sand **[J]**. Lightly finish with 400-grit paper.

Sand both sides of the ring. Look at the shank from all angles to make sure the sides are even **[K]**.

Add paste to the inside of the shank, if necessary. Dry. Sand the inside of the shank smooth, progressing up to 600-grit sandpaper.

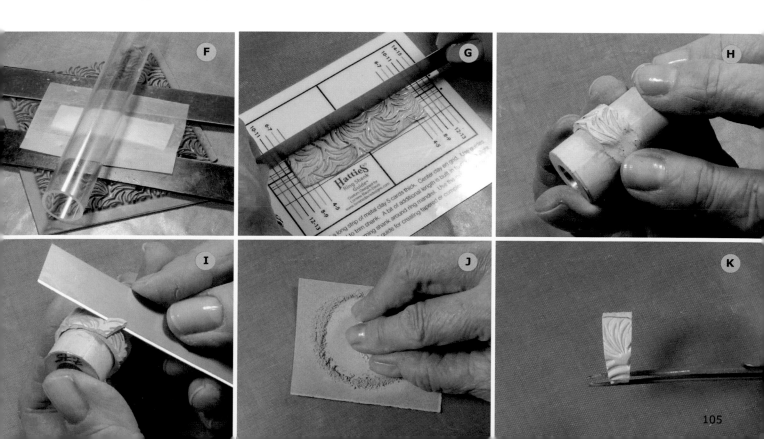

DAY 2

Do NOT use fiber paper. Vacuum your kiln if necessary. Dust and contaminants can mar the glass surface during firing.

Slump the glass

Remove the form and fused glass from the kiln. Use lapidary/glass machine tools or the coldworking files to shape the glass to about ½ x ¾" (12 x 18mm) (see instructions under "Coldwork the glass") **[L]**. You will refine the shape after the cab is slumped.

Clean the glass with isopropyl alcohol thoroughly before slumping. Coat the slumping form with kiln wash to prevent the glass from sticking. Apply five or six coats, allowing the kiln wash to dry thoroughly between coats. You can place the form in a toaster oven or dehydrator set to 200°F (93°C) to dry the wash.

Place the slumping form on the kiln shelf and put both into the kiln. Hold the fused glass at each end and balance it on the form, perpendicular to it.

Suggested schedule:
- R1 AFAP to 1300°F (704°C), hold 30 minutes
- R2 AFAP to 1370°F (743°C), hold 30 minutes
- R3 Off

Let the kiln return to room temperature and leave the glass in the kiln until it's completely cool to the touch.

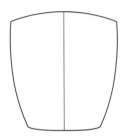

Template (actual size)

Make the ring side walls

> I like to use clear, colored plastic dividers from an office supply store for making templates. Thin, clear cutting mats from the dollar store work too. Color your template with a permanent marker so it's easy to find on your worktable.

Trace the template onto clear plastic and cut it out. Draw the center vertical line on the template.

> If the desired ring size is especially large, the bottom outside edges of the ring may not meet. You can leave this space open or fill it with clay and texture.

The ring walls' thickness is determined by the depth of the texture plates you use. These walls will extend beyond the shank

and need the bit of extra thickness that we've allowed.

Make the first wall and add the ring shank

Lightly oil the texture sheet, two nonstick plastic sheets, and two nonstick papers. Knead 20 grams of fresh clay for just a second or two and place it on the nonstick paper. It is helpful to shape the clay a bit before rolling to ensure you have enough clay for the template shape. Cover the clay with a plastic sheet protector and roll it to 8 cards/2mm thick. (Place the template over the clay to make sure it fits.)

Place the clay sheet on the texture sheet, cover it with a plastic sheet protector, and roll it to 6 cards/1.5mm thick. (I place slats alongside the clay, on top of the texture and under the binder plastic.) Gently lift off the plastic and gently place the template on top of the clay. Use the tissue blade to cut the clay following the template. Press down on the blade and push out and away from the template so you don't ruin the texture plate.

Lightly mark the center points on the top and bottom of the clay following the vertical line you marked on the template **[M]**. Carefully remove the template *without pulling the clay off the texture*. It is critical that you keep the clay on the texture; there is more to be done, and if the clay comes loose, you'll never be able to realign it with the texture sheet design.

Lightly indent the clay wall ¼" (7mm) from the top. Dampen one circular edge of the dried ring shank with water and add some diluted paste. Place the shank just below the mark you indent you made in the clay. Align the top and bottom marks on the wall with the top and bottom marks on the shank.

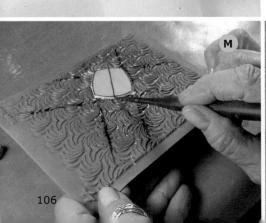

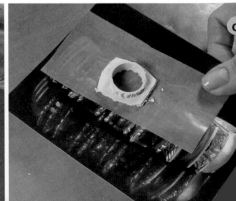

Lightly twist the shank a bit to get a really good bond. Make sure the widest part (top) of the shank is at the ¼" (7mm) mark. Again, align the center mark on the shank with the center mark on the wall. Make sure the ring is centered within the wall. Use a small damp paintbrush to smooth any extruded paste around the outside of the shank. Add paste where needed.

Immediately cut out the hole for the finger with a needle **[N]**. Use a damp paintbrush to smooth any extruded paste around the inside of the shank.

Carefully lift the ring off the texture, making sure the piece doesn't warp. Place it texture side down on parchment/nonstick paper and set aside to dry thoroughly **[O]**.

> To avoid warping en route to the drying station, place the ring and its paper on a postcard or index card.

Make the second wall of the ring. If the wall shank and assembly are still damp, cover the second textured wall on the texture sheet with plastic wrap and set aside. Wait until the former is dry and then proceed.

Add the second wall
Dampen the exposed edge of the dried ring shank with water and then with some diluted paste. Look directly over the top of the ring as you place the first wall over the second wall. The tops must be aligned, although they will not meet perfectly because the first wall is dry and the second is moist. The bottom portion of the ring can be shaped and sized later. Check the ring from all the angles. You can raise the texture sheet in your hand to get a better view **[P]**. Use a damp paintbrush to smooth any

extruded paste around the outside of the shank. Use a needle tool to cut out the hole for the finger. Use a damp paintbrush to smooth any extruded paste around the inside of the shank. If needed, use syringe clay or paste to fill any gaps at the joins. Dry thoroughly, making sure the sides do not distort in the move to the drying area. Sand inside the shank and up the top, sides, and bottom. Use fine files or micro carving tools to incise more texture on the sides, top, and bottom of the ring as desired **[Q]**.

The front gap, which will hold the cab, should be at least ⁵⁄₁₆" (8mm) wide. To make a jig to check the opening, glue four craft sticks together. Lightly oil the outside surfaces of the jig. Set it in the slot **[S]**. If the opening isn't even, heavily dampen the inside surface of the top walls and let the assembly set until fairly damp throughout but not wet in the slot area.

Place the jig inside and hold together with your fingers for about 3 minutes. To avoid damaging the texture, don't get any moisture on the outside surfaces. This trick will avoid an uneven top view.

DAY 3
Coldwork the glass, assemble, and fire
Use safety measures every time you work with the glass: Use eye protection and dust masks.

Put water in the bowl. Keep the sanding surface of the glass wet at all times by repeatedly dipping the file into the water.

File the glass on both sides starting with the coarsest grit (120) **[S]**. Use this file until the work is nearly the right size. Use a 200-grit file until the right size is reached.

To finish the fused glass, you'll need glass coldworking files in various grits, a small bowl of water, and safety glasses.

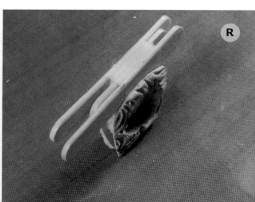

107

Remember that the cab sides have to be on an angle to accommodate the slant of the ring walls. The ends of the cab need to be a bit narrower than the top because the glass will slump some during firing and the wall openings get narrower farther away from the top.

Be sure the glass cabochon fits loosely, but not sloppily, in the channel **[T]**. This will accommodate the shrinkage of the metal clay as it sinters. Turn the cabochon 180 degrees to determine the best way it fits in the slot.

Set the cabochon

Wash your hands. Clean the cabochon with the swab dipped in isopropyl alcohol. Wipe dry. Apply a generous amount of overlay paste in the center of the slot of the ring. Center the cabochon securely. Dry completely.

Fire the ring

You'll sinter the ring and fire-polish the cabochon simultaneously. You can anticipate the movement of the glass as it heats; usually glass will reform to ¼" (7mm) high and its edges will round. The height of this cab will not change because of the fuse firing.

Carefully prop the ring upright in the can of silica sand or cut a slice in the middle of a thick fiber blanket square and set the ring into the slot **[U]**. Place the propped ring on the kiln shelf. Hold the shelf up to eye level and view from several sides to make sure the ring is perpendicular to the shelf.

Moving slowly and carefully to cut down on dust movement, put the shelf on the kiln stilts and close the kiln door.

Suggested sintering and fire-polishing schedule

- Ramp to hold
- R1 AFAP 1400°F (760°C) 20 minutes
- R2 AFAP 960°F (516°C) 60 minutes
- R3 AFAP 150°F (66°C) off

Allow the kiln to cool to room temperature. After the ring is totally cool, brass brush it in soapy water. Tumble-polish, rinse, and dry.

Lora Hart, Parapet Ring, 2008. Fine silver, sterling silver, felt, carnelian, patina. Photo by Marsha Thomas.

Ivy Solomon Coneflower, 2011. Sterling silver, fine silver, colored resin, sand. Photo by Steve Solomon.

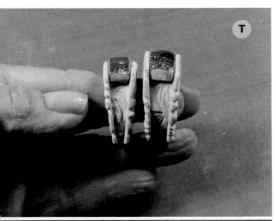

About the contributors

JANET ALEXANDER has more than 35 years of experience in jewelry metal arts as a bench jeweler, designer, and instructor. She has demonstrated her lost wax casting and wax carving techniques on television, and her work has been published in *American Craft* magazine, *Metal Clay Artist* magazine, and the book *New Directions: Powder Metallurgy in a Sheet Metal World*. Janet has a BFA in metals from the University of North Texas and has studied metalworking with several master jewelers. She has GIA certification in diamond grading and stone setting. Additionally, she has certification in Precious Metal Clay with Rio Grande, crossover certification with Art Clay, and is a PMC Connection senior instructor and technical advisor.
janetalexander.net
thejewelryclassroom.com

LORENA ANGULO grew up in Mexico, and her work reflects the time she spent absorbing the traditions of beautiful Mexican folk art. She creates most of her wearable artwork using only a carving tool, a needle tool, and her hands. Lorena is on the faculty of San Antonio's Southwest School of Art metals department. Lorena's work has been featured in several publications of the Precious Metal Clay Guild as well as in books, magazines, and countless online articles and industry websites. Lorena was a juror for the PMC Annual 5 along with Robert Ebendorf, Celie Fago, and Kelly Russell. Lorena creates her unique jewelry in silver, copper, and bronze at her studio in San Antonio, Texas.
lorenaangulo.com

LORRENE BAUM-DAVIS' mother instilled a love of the ceramic arts and her father introduced her to ferrous metals by teaching her to weld and use a lathe at a young age. Lorrene graduated from the Revere Academy of Jewelry Arts in San Francisco and has been on their faculty. Lorrene is one of nine master instructors with Art Clay World USA. Many of her workshops are held at her Sierra Foothills Studio in Placerville, California. She is the author of *Setting Gemstones in Metal Clay* (2007). She was a featured speaker, teacher, and demonstrator at several Metal Clay World Conferences. She has won numerous awards, including three in 2011 for her Legends series of rings, which are featured in this book. Lorrene is also a theater actress and director.
lorrenedavisdesigns.com

MAGGIE BERGMAN is credited with introducing photopolymer plates to the metal clay community; today they are a widely used tool for adding texture. She was one of 15 advisors worldwide that helped set up the metal clay Masters Registry in 2007. Maggie continues her work with traditional metals as well as metal clay and teaches from her studio in S.E. Queensland, Australia.
silverclayart.com

PAT BOLGAR has participated in art and craft festivals throughout the United States since 1990. She studied printmaking and fashion design, and strives to create jewelry that pairs individuality with wearability. She works with polymer, metal clays, sterling silver, and objects from nature. Her jewelry is featured in several books, magazines, and many gallery exhibitions, including two traveling exhibits sponsored by Ohio Designer Craftsmen. In 2007, she was a finalist for the Saul Bell Design Award in the PMC category.
patbolgar.com

BARBARA BRIGGS is an award-winning artist who works in mixed media, including polymer and precious metal clay, chain mail, resin, and bead weaving. She has designed and marketed patterns for numerous art projects and written articles which have been published in *Bead&Button* and *Metal Clay Artist* magazines. Barbara has more than 20 years of metalsmithing experience and is PMC certified.
barbarabriggsdesigns.com

SANDRA BUTCHKO grew up in a very artistic family. She credits her 10th grade ceramics teacher with instilling a love of clay and placing her on the path that became her life's work. She discovered metal clay quite by accident in 1999, and by 2001, she was a certified senior instructor for Art Clay USA. She now has a level 3 certification in PMC as well. Sandra runs a

custom tool and mold design manufacturing company called Cottontail Creations in Ventura, California. "Every day is a new adventure with this medium," Sandra says. "I look forward to all the new discoveries to come."
cottontailcreations.net

PAM EAST is an internationally known artist, writer, and teacher from Atlanta. She has been an enamelist since 1997 and was named a master instructor for Art Clay Silver in 2005. Pam has demonstrated her techniques on television, and her work and instructional articles have appeared in *Art Jewelry* magazine, *Metal Clay Artist* magazine, and many others. Her book, *Enameling on Metal Clay*, is available in bookstores and online. Pam has also been an invited speaker, giving classes and lectures at the Enamelist Society Biennial Conference, the Metal Clay World Conference, and the Pan-European Metal Clay Festival.
pameast.net

JOY FUNNELL, from Hastings, UK, is a craftsman of the Guild of Enamellers and a senior instructor for Art Clay. She teaches silver clay and enameling-on-silver workshops from her home base and travels to teach throughout the UK and abroad. She is passionate about using textures and color in her work and specializes in her "enameled accents" technique. Her award-winning work has been published in various magazines and books, including the cover of *Metal Clay Artist* magazine. She taught at several Art Clay World UK Conferences, the Guild of Enamellers Conference, and the 2011 Metal Clay World Conference.
joyfunnell.co.uk

VICKIE HALLMARK works from her home studio in Austin, Texas. Trained as a scientist, she studied silver and gold surfaces with laser beams and atomic resolution microscopes. Now she uses that background to inform her artistic experiments with metal clay. Her avian-themed jewelry has appeared in print in *Metal Clay Artist* magazine, PMC Guild

Annuals 4 and 5, *Metal Clay Today*, The Art and Design of Metal Clay Jewelry Calendar, and her self-published book, *Birdwatching*. Vickie loves to combine metal with colored resin or hand-painted glass. Her glass endeavors have been profiled in *Bead&Button* magazine, *The Glass Bead*, and *The Flow* magazine.
vickiehallmark.com

HADAR JACOBSON is a jewelry artist and instructor who has been exploring metal clay for the past 15 years. She lives and works in Berkeley, California, and teaches workshops all over the world. Her work and articles have been published over the years in many books and professional magazines. She has published four books about metal clay. She also manufactures metal clays in powder form, including copper, bronze, and steel alloys, and currently specializes in mixed-metal jewelry and patterns of color in metal clay. Her popular blog, an ongoing tutorial on metal clay, features articles, instructions and discoveries.
hadarjacobson.com

PATRICIA KIMLE has been involved in art from childhood on. Her early interests focused on apparel design and later, jewelry. Patricia holds a Ph.D. in textiles and clothing. She has been exploring polymer clay for over 20 years. In 2004, she began to add metal clay to the mixture to create mixed-media jewelry. Patricia sells her jewelry to galleries and gift shops across the country. In her work, she uses original drawings, carved designs, and molds of foliage collected in her own yard in her artwork. Patricia has written more than 30 project articles for jewelry craft magazines and general craft publications. She teaches polymer and metal clay at events around the country, including the Bead&Button Show. She is the author of *Polymer Clay Inspirations*, *Perfectly Paired: Designing Jewelry with Polymer and Metal Clay*, and an upcoming book about creating polymer clay canes.
kimledesigns.com

IRINA MIECH has always loved to create with her hands. Metal clay allows her to explore new paths because it's so well-suited to organic work and designs with natural elements. She teaches jewelry design classes at her retail bead store, Eclectica, as well as the Bead&Button Show. She began her own metal clay certification program in 2007. She is the author of eight jewelry design books and many of her jewelry designs have been featured in publications including *Bead&Button*, *Bead Style*, and *Art Jewelry* magazines.
eclecticabeads.com

KIM OTTERBEIN has worked with metal clay since 1998 and has made jewelry since she was 5 years old. She and her husband own the Bead House and Metal Arts Studio in Bristol, Rhode Island, where Kim offers more than 50 different classes in beading, wirework, metal clay, polymer clay, and metalsmithing. Her favorite way of making jewelry is combining different media.
thebeadhouse.com

CATHERINE DAVIES PAETZ is a jewelry artist and metalsmith working primarily in metal clay, often incorporating 24k gold, enamel, beads, or pearls into her designs. She has been creating jewelry for more than 35 years and has a BFA in metals and enameling. As a certified PMC artisan and instructor, Catherine regularly teaches classes and workshops, and has presented seminars and demonstrations at PMC conferences. She is recognized as a leader in the development of water etching on metal clay and wrote a book on that technique. She has written several metal clay technique articles, images of her work have appeared in numerous books and magazines, and her jewelry is sold in galleries and at fine craft shows.
cdpdesigns.com

CINDY PANKOPF teaches jewelry making from her studio/shop called Cindy Pankopf's Creative Place in Fullerton, California, and at workshops across the country, including the Bead&Button Show. Cindy has attained the master level of certification with Art Clay World USA and is certified to teach with PMC products as well. She is the author of the books *The Absolute Beginners Guide: Making Metal Clay Jewelry* and *BeadMaille*. Cindy's beadwork and metal clay designs have won awards in *Bead&Button* magazine's BeadDreams competition.
cindypankopf.com

CINDY SILAS is an award-winning designer and certified metal clay instructor who creates limited edition and one-of-a-kind art jewelry in mixed media, particularly metal clay, polymer, and resin. She loves a good "what if" challenge, which has led to numerous discoveries and innovations. Cindy's jewelry and techniques have been published in *Art Jewelry* magazine, *Metal Clay Artist* magazine, PMC Fusion, the PMC Guild Annual, and The Art and Design of Metal Clay Jewelry calendar, among others. She is working on a book that celebrates the combination of metal clay and polymer.
cindysilas.com

SUSAN BREEN SILVY is a metal clay and glass bead artist and past president of the International Society of Glass Beadmakers. Her work has been exhibited extensively in juried and invitational exhibitions nationally and at the Silver Accessories Exhibition in Tokyo, Japan. She has received numerous awards including first place in both the Lapidary Journal Bead Arts Award and *Bead&Button* magazine's BeadDreams Exhibition. Her piece Industrial Chic was a finalist in the metal clay category of the 2012 Saul Bell Design award competition. Her work has been published in numerous magazines and books. She lives in Kansas City, Missouri, and teaches at the Kansas City Art Institute. Her work can be found in the permanent collection of the Missouri Governor's Mansion and the Bead Museum in Washington, D.C.
susanbreensilvy.com

JEWELYN VANONI has been working with metal clay and inspiring students across the country since 2000. Since 2004, she has been a part of the design and invention team for her family's business, Cottontail Creations, creating new tools and molds for the metal clay community. Her background is in ceramics, and she spent a number of years working with hot glass and polymer clay. Jewelyn is a regular contributor to *Art Jewelry* magazine.
cottontailcreations.net

MICHELA VERANI is an artist who works in metal clay, felt, and fused glass. Her love of the natural world is the inspiration for her metal clay pieces. She tries to give voice to the spirit and cycle of nature: the growth of vegetation, the relationship of its creatures to one another, or the beauty of a day. She has achieved Art Clay Level 1/senior certification, Rio Rewards certification, is a juried member of the League of New Hampshire Craftsmen in metal clay, and was the seventh person to pass jurying for the Metal Clay Master's Registry II. Michela's jewelry has won awards and has been featured in a number of PMC Guild Annuals and books on jewelry. She has authored articles for many periodicals. She teaches metal clay primarily at her home studio in Londonderry, N.H., and Metalwerx School of Jewelry and Metal Arts in Waltham, Mass.. Her work is sold in local galleries, as well as by commission.
everlastingtreasures.org

Compiling editor **MARY WOHLGEMUTH** is a senior editor for Kalmbach Books who specializes in topics for metalsmiths.

A note on process photography
All step-by-step photos were taken by the designers, with these exceptions:
Metal leaf magic by Sandra Butchko and **Medusa's garden** by Jewelyn Vanoni: process photos by Jason Cory Clay
Fantasy flower by Irina Miech: process photos by James Forbes
Polymer petals by Pat Bolgar: process photos by Kevin Olds

Sources and resources

Here are recommendations for references that expand on some of the topics covered in this book, as well as suggestions for finding some of the more unusual supplies used in the projects.

For an introduction to working with metal clay:
The Absolute Beginners Guide: Making Metal Clay Jewelry by Cindy Thomas Pankopf

For more information on the tearaway technique:
Keum-Boo on Silver by Celie Fago

Full-spectrum impact (p. 12)
Dye oxides: sculptnouveau.com or cforiginals.net (the Swellegants line includes dye oxides)

Filled frame beads (p. 16)
Frames: singarajaimports.com

Metal leaf magic (p. 19)
Sea turtle mold: wholelottawhimsy.com

Golden arrows (p. 29)
Triangle template: Isomars #2155, isomars.com

Mokume gane daisy (p. 37)
Clays and firing instructions that apply to most brands: hadarjacobson.com/blog

Luminosity (p. 44)
Starburst Collection texture sheet: rollingmillresource.etsy.com; Cattelya enamels: zamauk.com; Toho enamels: enamelemporium.com

Beaded leaf (p. 60)
Enamel, lily root powder: enamelworksupply.com

Textured feathers (p. 64)
Thermal negative film: wholelottawhimsy.com; thick plates: boxcarpress.com (by special request)

Brilliant fibula (p. 70)
Wax resist: maycocolors.com, aftosa.com, or amaco.com

Resin window (p. 87)
Pickett Combo Ellipse Master template: utrechtart.com or dickblick.com

Enameled riverbed (p. 97)
Lead-free enamels: thompsonenamel.com

Legends rings (p. 103)
Ring shank guide: hattiesanderson.com
For further reading about working with glass:
A Beginner's Guide to Kiln-Formed Glass, Brenda Griffith, and *Coldworking Glass Without Machines*, Paul Tarlow

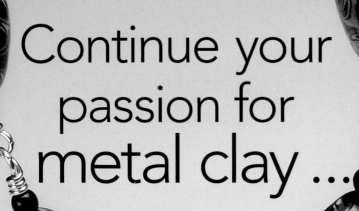

Continue your passion for metal clay ...

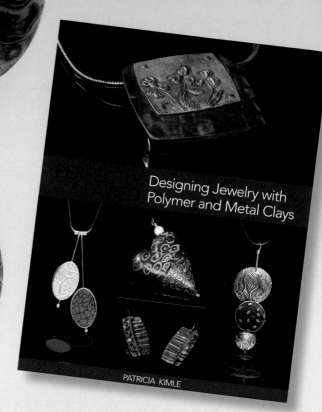

Designing Jewelry with Polymer and Metal Clays

PATRICIA KIMLE

Perfectly Paired: Designing Jewelry with Polymer and Metal Clays

Patricia Kimle opens up a world of creativity by combining two unique elements in a variety of projects. Learn her insider's secrets for pairing the color and pattern of polymer clay with the texture and structure of metal clay. The end result showcases each medium at its best!

62946 • $21.95

KALMBACH BOOKS

Buy now from your favorite bead or craft shop!

Or at **www.KalmbachStore.com**
or call 1-800-533-6644

Monday – Friday, 8:30 a.m. – 4:30 p.m. CST. Outside the United States and Canada call 262-796-8776, ext. 661.

 www.facebook.com/KalmbachJewelryBooks

 www.twitter.com/KalmbachBooks

P16636